The world
is full of scavengers,
but most of them would rather

kill

their own food than find it

at least prefer their *trouvailles* to be fresh as possible

and turn up their noses

at carcasses

in advanced stages of

putrefaction.

don't have the stomach for them.

Vultures
do.

WAYNE GRADY

L

Sierra Club Books

San Francisco

E

Nature's Ghastly Gourmet

EDITING: Nancy Flight
JACKET AND BOOK DESIGN: Tom Brown
FRONT JACKET PHOTOGRAPH:
Art Wolfe/Tony Stone Images
ILLUSTRATIONS: Roxanna Bikadoroff

Printed and bound in Hong Kong by C&C Offset

The Sierra Club, founded in 1892 by John Muir, has devoted itself to the study and protection of the Earth's scenic and ecological resources—mountains, wetlands, woodlands, wild shores and rivers, deserts and plains. The publishing program of the Sierra Club offers books to the public as a nonprofit educational service in the hope that they may enlarge the public's understanding of the Club's basic concerns. The point of view expressed in each book, however, does not necessarily represent that of the Club. The Sierra Club has some sixty chapters coast to coast, in Canada, Hawaii, and Alaska. For information about how you may participate in its programs to preserve wilderness and the quality of life, please address inquiries to Sierra Club, 85 Second Street, San Francisco, CA 94105

http://www.sierraclub.org/books

Originally published in Canada by Greystone Books, a division of Douglas & McIntyre, Ltd., 1615 Venables Street, Vancouver, BC V5L 2H1.

LIBRARY OF CONGRESS CATALOGUING-
IN-PUBLICATION DATA

Grady, Wayne.
  Vulture: nature's ghastly gourmet/by Wayne Grady
        p.   cm.
  Includes bibliographical references and index.
  ISBN 0-87156-982-5 (alk. paper)
  1. Vultures. I. Title
QL696.F3G72 1997
598.9'2- -dc21   97-7182
                                               CIP

10 9 8 7 6 5 4 3 2 1

"Black Vulture," on p. 56, is from *The Art of Birds* by Pablo Neruda, translated by Jack Schmitt, copyright © 1985. Used by permission of the University of Texas Press.
Every attempt has been made to trace accurate ownership of copyrighted visual material in this book. Errors and omissions will be corrected in subsequent editions, provided notification is sent to the publisher.

CONTENTS

One

by one,

there flapped heavily out of

the branches dark,

hideou

birds,

with fierce hooked claws and

featherless

heads and

necks

EDGAR
ALLAN POE
MADE A FINE CASE FOR
THE SAGACITY OF RAVENS, BUT HE
WAS NO FRIEND OF THE VULTURE. IN "THE RAVEN,"
he describes the bird, at least at first, as "a stately Raven of the saintly days of yore." The poor vulture receives no such treatment in Poe's hands, for in "The Tell-Tale Heart," Poe's hero murders an old man for no better reason than that "he had the eye of a vulture . . . a dull blue, with a hideous veil over it that chilled the very marrow in my bones."

Though an innovative writer in most other ways, in his vituperation of vultures Poe was following an old tradition. The Bible called them "an abomination." Charles Darwin, in *The Voyage of the Beagle*, referred to the turkey vulture as "a disgusting bird, with its bald scarlet head formed to wallow in putridity." We reserve epithets for the vulture that we would not bestow on any other creature in nature. When newspaper headlines announce, as one in the Toronto *Globe and Mail* recently did, that following an economic débâcle in Europe "vulture investors swoop on France," we know exactly what they mean.

Why this malice towards vultures? It cannot be simply that vultures are scavengers, for many animals scavenge that otherwise evoke our admiration. Eagles will land on a carcass and eat it; a biologist I know puts dead chickens at the top of a 6-metre (20-foot) pole to attract red-tailed hawks; the white admiral (*Limenitis arthemis*) is by all accounts a beautiful butterfly that feeds on nectar when it can get it, but it is also, according to entomologist Alexander Klots, "addicted to carrion, excrement and the secretions of aphids." Much of the food eaten by coyotes, hyenas, skunks, crows and gulls has been killed for them by some other animal. Even the sainted raven, Poe's pet, is a ghoulish gourmet in its own right: John James Audubon, writing around the same time as Poe, describes a killing flood on the Mississippi River, after which could be heard "the dismal scream of an Eagle or a Raven . . . as the foul bird rises, disturbed by your approach, from the carcass on which it was allaying its craving appetite." And yet we don't abhor eagles and ravens.

It hasn't always been thus. In ancient times, the vulture was revered: in pre-dynastic Egypt it was identified with the goddess Nekhbet and was the symbol of the upper kingdom; in India, vultures guarded the gates to the underworld. And in the pre-Columbian New World, the vulture occupied a place equivalent to that of the jaguar in South America and its nemesis the raven in West Coast Native mythology: it was, after all, the California condor that gave shape and meaning to the iconography of the Thunderbird.

It is my hope that this book will restore to the vulture the positive image it once enjoyed in human legend and undo the bad press it has received in more modern times. We have begun, I think, to look upon nature and its creatures with a degree of acceptance at least approaching that of the ancients—we see this in efforts to restore the gray wolf to its former range, in campaigns to save the cougar and the grizzly and the beluga, and in the story, told in the last chapter of this book, of the long, difficult struggle to pull the California and Andean condors back from the brink of extinction. In *The Practice of the Wild*, poet and essayist Gary Snyder imagines a "depth ecology" that would include the darker side of nature, "the ball of crunched bones in a scat, the feathers in the snow, the tales of insatiable appetite." The vulture inhabits such a wild system. "Human beings," says Snyder, "have made much of purity and are repelled by blood, pollution, putrefaction." But we must learn to accept all of nature if we are to live with any of it, for it does not come by halves.

There are strong movements in political and corporate circles these days to reduce the power of the Environmental Protection Act (EPA) in both the United States and Canada in the name of economic growth. In both North and South America, setting aside habitat vital to native species is seen as an impediment to rather than a measure of civilization. Battles that began in John Muir's day and seemed won with the passing of the EPA in the 1970s are everywhere being rejoined as if they had never taken place. May this book encourage us to reexamine our attitude towards vultures and condors in particular, as we must reexamine our attitude towards nature in general, and help us to make room in our hearts for all creatures, no matter how they make their living. Let us look at the treatment we have meted out to vultures and say, with Poe's pardoned raven, "Nevermore!"

THERE ARE
A GREAT MANY
PEOPLE INVOLVED IN VULTURE
AND CONDOR RESEARCH IN NORTH AND

SOUTH AMERICA, AND THIS BOOK OWES A DEBT OF gratitude to all of them. Those who have been particularly helpful include Mike Wallace of the Los Angeles Zoo, who read the early manuscript and made many valuable comments; David Kirk, who gladly shared his research on turkey and black vultures in Venezuela with me at his home in Quebec; and Kent Prior, of Carleton University, whose work on turkey vulture foraging habits in Ontario provided many insights into the nature of that fascinating bird. Adrian Forsyth was an important early influence on my interest in vultures. Others who have been of assistance as informants, counsellors and listeners include David Bird, Martin Silverstone, Brian Brett, Farley Mowat and Harry Thurston; my gratitude and friendship extends to them all.

Candace Savage has exerted her usual wise and calming influence on my efforts to transform raw research into polished prose. My editor, Nancy Flight, valiantly wrestled the book through its successive drafts, and the designer, Tom Brown, created a wonderful design for the book. I would also like to thank Kathleen Shelton for her help during the research stage of the project and Leah Jahn for her valuable editorial assistance.

And, once again, my everlasting thanks to Merilyn Simonds for her patient and inspiriting presence.

The Value of Vultures

Know ye the land where the cypress and myrtle
e emblems of deeds that are done in their clime?
Where the rage of the vulture, the love of the turtle
Now melt into sorrow, now madden to crime!

— BYRON, "The Bride of Abydos"

I

ON

A PLEASANT

SUMMER MORNING

IN 1889, TWO WOMEN WALKED

TO THE TOP OF MALABAR HILL, ABOVE BOMBAY, to attend the funeral of a small child who had died in the city during the night. One of them was Sara Jeannette Duncan, a Canadian travel writer and journalist; her companion, also a journalist, was Lily Lewis. The women were travelling around the world, financing their trip by sending reports back to the *Montreal Star* and the *Washington Post*, and they thought that witnessing a traditional Parsee funeral would give them something interesting to write home about. They were not disappointed.

Arriving just ahead of the funeral procession, they were shown by a white-turbaned monk into a beautiful walled garden that looked down over the city and the wide blue expanse of the bay. Their attention, however, was not drawn to the flowers or the city or the sunrise, Duncan later wrote, but to "five strange round, white structures that rose at a little distance, divided from us by a wall, in the midst of heavy masses of trees."

These were the famed Towers of Silence, in use in Asia

African white-backed vultures (*Gyps africanus*) roost on a dead acacia tree in the Kalahari.
DANIEL J. COX/NATURAL EXPOSURES

since the 6th century A.D., when the Persian mystic Zoroaster first laid down the rules for the cleansing ceremony that was a Parsee funeral. Although Duncan and Lewis had heard about these peculiar "Sky Burials," as they were called, they were still vague about what to expect. Duncan understood that the towers had something to do with purification — "they were not vaults, and they were not cemeteries," she knew, "yet their business was with the dead." But she had not guessed their true purpose. Were they funeral pyres, she wondered?

While the rest of the procession was still out of sight over the brow of the hill, the two women became aware of a commotion that seemed to come from the trees near the towers. They watched in growing agitation, she wrote, as

> one by one, there flapped heavily out of the branches dark, hideous birds, with fierce hooked claws and featherless heads and necks. They began to come in twos and threes, then in half-dozens, and settled closely together in high-shouldered rows, heads looking over, along the top of the stone parapet of the nearest tower. They knew the funeral was coming long before we did.

The hideous birds were vultures, and the women were about to experience one of the most gruesome and horrifying scenes of their lives. As they watched, the procession made its way through a narrow doorway in the side of the nearest of the five Towers of Silence. By now, they had begun to suspect what it was they were about to see:

> The vultures above crowded together more thickly, and stretched out their evil heads. The corpse-bearers entered with their burden; the mourners turned back and went into one of the Sagri, the prayer houses, where the sacred fire burns incense and sandal wood all day and all night, to pray.
>
> A moment, and then all the air seemed full of the flapping of dark wings, and hoarse cries, and the parapet was quite empty. We turned away in unspeakable loathing, angry that we had come, and unable to rid ourselves of the imaginative carnage behind the great round wall....

Duncan never did learn what had taken place inside the tower between the time the mourners entered the prayer house and the time the vultures left their perches on the tower's parapet. The principal mourner, a respected friend of the child's family, would have set the body on a stone altar in the lower chamber of the tower and, while the family looked on, proceeded to hack the dead child to pieces with an axe. That accomplished, he and an assistant would have carried the pieces up to the tower roof — actually a large metal grid spanning the chamber's ceiling — and placed them on the grid. That's when the vultures would have descended. Within half an hour, there would have been nothing left of the dead child but a scattering of bones and a skull.

Sky Burials are still common in India — an almost identical scene to that witnessed by Duncan is described in Rohinton Mistry's novel *Such a Long Journey*, set in Bombay in 1971. And they are still daily occurrences at the Sera Monastery in Lhasa, Tibet. On a flat rock above the lamasery, Sky Burials take place every day except Sunday; foreigners—particularly foreigners with cameras — are discouraged from attending them, but several accounts have been published in the West. One, which appeared in the *Vancouver Sun* in 1985, describes a ritual that was even more horrible to watch than the funeral witnessed by Duncan.

It involved two bodies. Both were stripped and dismembered by two undertakers, each attendant working on a single body, "hacking the flesh and muscles into chunks with meat cleavers and knives and tossing the bones into a pile. Two attendants pounded the bones into dust with heavy hammers while loudly chanting Buddhist prayers." The bone meal was then mixed with yak's milk and barley flour and poured over the piles of flesh so that nothing would be left when the vultures had finished:

> The vultures rip pieces of meat out of each other's beaks, madly competing until there is no more food. The huge birds are fat and sleek, white feathers that adorn their heads and necks make them appear similar to American bald eagles.

Buddhists, unlike Parsees, view a funeral not as a cleansing of the earth but as the passage of the body into a purer state, a kind of reunion with the cosmos:

"Buddhism," a Tibetan lama explained to the *Sun* correspondent, "teaches that you should give yourself to others and to nature during your life. So it is natural to give yourself to the birds when you die."

Vilifying Vultures

THE BIRDS TAKING PART IN THE SKY BURIAL WERE PROBABLY Himalayan griffons (*Gyps himalayensis*); large, pale brown vultures with long, white, featherless necks, they soar on high mountain thermals looking for fallen goats or stillborn sheep. Or they may have been Indian black vultures (*Sarcogyps calvus*). Known in Hindu mythology as the gatekeepers of hell — one hunches on either side of the gate, eyeing entrants for their suitability — Indian black vultures are the largest species of vulture in Asia, with red, almost transparent skin covering their bony heads and necks. Griffon vultures (*Gyps fulvus*), highly sociable scavengers that feed, roost and even nest in groups of thirty or more, have also been known to partake in the Parsee ritual.

By even the most liberal standard of beauty, vultures — at least on the ground — are not beautiful. Their bald heads and bare, serpentlike necks are too readily associated with death and decay; their featherlessness enables them to slide their heads into the inner reaches of putrid carcasses without having to spend a lot of time grooming afterwards. "The naked skin on the head of a vulture," noted Charles Darwin in *The Origin of Species*, "is generally considered as a direct adaptation for wallowing in putridity; and so it may be, or it may possibly be due to the direct action of putrid matter. . . ." Either way, vultures test our unconditional love of nature. Their wattles are the colour of glistening gore; their baleful eyes remind us of the horrors they have beheld. Vultures in art and literature are always harbingers of imminent demise. Circling vultures over a desert landscape tell us immediately that some movie star just over the rise is dying of thirst. In the novel *The Vulture*, by British writer Catherine Heath, a vulture is kept as a pet by a breeder of thoroughbred hunting dogs, and we know that by the end of the book one of those prize canines is going to that great kennel in the sky minus a few body parts. Heath describes the pet vulture as being not only repulsive, but repulsive in an almost human way: "It did not look like a bird," she writes. "It looked like a huddle of old rags

White-backs in Kenya may wheel above a carcass to communicate their find to other vultures.

DANIEL J. COX/NATURAL EXPOSURES

thrown over a naked body, whose stringy neck and red head stuck out at the top as if surveying a hostile world from a safe shelter."

Vultures are the bottom feeders of the bird world. Little wonder that vultures have long been regarded as unclean in the Middle East. "And these are they which ye shall have in abomination among the fowls," warns the author of *Leviticus* (11: 13 –14); "they shall not be eaten, they are an abomination: the eagle, and the ossifrage, and the ospray, and the vulture. . . ."

The biblical mandate is levied against virtually all winged carnivores — it also includes kites, ravens, owls, nighthawks, cormorants, swans (which eat mostly aquatic plants but will occasionally swallow an insect), pelicans, storks, herons and even bats. Even so, the poor vulture comes in for special opprobrium: the Hebrew word for eagle, *nesher*, is the same as the word for vulture, and "ossifrage," from the Latin *ossifraga*, meaning "bone-breaker," is an old name for the bearded vulture (*Gypaëtus barbatus*), one of the most common species of North Africa and Europe. Osprey, the name now given to the fish hawk, is an anglicized corruption of "ossifrage."

The **Vulture** in Egypt

• IN PREDYNASTIC EGYPT, when the country was divided into Upper and Lower Egypt, the goddess of Upper Egypt was Nekhbet. Her sacred animal was the vulture; she was sometimes portrayed as a divinity with the bald head of a vulture, hovering over the head of the Pharaoh. Nekhbet's cult was centred in Nekhen, which later became El Kab, and the Egyptian vulture was prominently depicted in shrines devoted to her worship.

The white crown of Upper Egypt worn by Nekhbet was a stylized vulture; the red crown of Lower Egypt carried the cobra, or *uraeus*, the symbol of Nekhbet's counterpart, Buto. When the two   >>>

Venerating Vultures

THE OLD WORLD ATTITUDE TOWARDS VULtures was, however, deliciously ambiguous. On the one hand, vultures were vilified for their ugliness and disgusting eating habits; on the other hand, citizens appreciated the vulture's role in ridding the landscape of disease-bearing corpses. The ambiguity shows up most clearly in the association of vultures with war and its aftermath. Ancient historians tell of skies darkened by flocks of vultures following armies into battle. Archaeologists in the city of Catal Huyuk, in Anatolia, have unearthed a Vulture Chamber dating from 6200 B.C., one wall

>>> Egypts were united under one Pharaoh, the combined crown included a vulture and a cobra, symbolizing the union of Upper and Lower Egypt. The golden mask of Tutankhamen shows a vulture above the king's right eye and a cobra above his left.

Nekhbet was also the goddess of childbirth, and she was often depicted suckling the Pharaoh; she is therefore associated with another Egyptian deity, Mut—who was later identified by the Greeks with their most powerful goddess, Hera. Mut is an ill-defined deity but is usually depicted wearing the vulture headdress, and the hieroglyph for her name—a vulture—also signified "mother." >>>

of which is decorated with a painting showing seven vultures hovering over six ritually decapitated captive soldiers. The Stele of the Vultures, a stone column erected in Mesopotamia by Eannatum in 2650 B.C., also depicts heaped bodies of slain enemies being avidly torn asunder by vultures. The Stone of Susa, erected in 2300 B.C. by Sargon I, king of ancient Elam (part of modern Iran), shows much the same thing: enemy corpses and hovering vultures. The vulture, not the eagle, symbolized the outcome of war: no matter which side won, the spoils always went to the vulture.

In 1758, Samuel Johnson published a short essay in *The Idler* called "The Vulture," telling of a Bohemian shepherd who, "by long abode in the forests, enabled himself to understand the voice of birds," and who claimed to have once overheard a female vulture instructing her offspring "in the arts of a vulture's life." These arts were primarily those of finding food, and the easiest way to find food, she told them, was to look for the place where armies were waging war: "When you hear noise and see fire which flashes along the ground, hasten to the place with your swiftest wing, for men are surely destroying one another; you will then find the ground smoking with blood and covered with carcasses, of which many are dismembered and mangled for the convenience of vultures." Man, the old vulturess concluded, with his penchant for self-destruction, "shews by his eagerness and diligence that he is, more than any of the others, a friend to vultures."

The ancient Egyptians honoured vultures in word as well as in deed. In predynastic Egypt, the vulture hieroglyph stood for the entire region of Egypt south of Thebes, just as the cobra, or *uraeus*, was the emblem of the north. The hieroglyph for the Egyptian goddess Nekhbet, daughter of Ra and "creatrix of the world," was a vulture: she is also depicted in Egyptian art wearing a headdress consisting of a stylized white crown fringed with vulture feathers, and her capital, the town of Nekhen, was the centre of a vast vulture cult, focussed

OVERLEAF:
A white-backed
vulture competes
with two hyenas
for a lion-killed
Cape buffalo
carcass in Kenya.
ERWIN AND PEGGY BAUER

in the sanctuary of "the venerable vulture," which con-
tained images of the Egyptian vulture (*Neophron perc-
nopterus*). During the time of the Pharaohs, when the
northern and southern kingdoms were united under a
single ruler, the Pharaoh's headdress consisted of Nekhbet's vulture crown sur-
mounted by a cobra: south and north in coalition. The Egyptian vulture was
protected by law — it became known as "Pharaoh's chicken" — the first legal
protection ever accorded a wild animal. And because it was believed that only
female Egyptian vultures existed — they were impregnated by the south or
southeastern winds — the birds came to symbolize absolute independent
authority: feminine nature unhampered by interference from outside itself.

The Remains of the Day

WHY ARE THE REST OF US SO DOWN ON
vultures? Some of the reasons are purely sensorial.
Vultures stink. There is an air of the graveyard
about them. Although vultures prefer to nest near
water, and wash themselves meticulously after
gorging on a rotted carcass, they don't always get
it all off. Startled baby vultures, which feed on carcasses regurgitated for them by their parents, hiss
at intruders, and their hiss functions much as the
spray of a skunk. Really startled vultures vomit, as
camels do, except that vulture vomit is composed
of stuff no camel could imagine.

We value our sense of smell, which is intricately linked to our sense of taste. If, while blindfolded,
we hold an orange to our noses and eat a piece of
apple, the apple will taste like an orange. We trust
our noses; when they tell us something is putrid,
our brains tell us not to eat it. Those deprived of a
sense of smell, a physiological condition known as
anosmia, also have no sense of taste and run the risk
of eating food that their noses ought to have told

>>> Vultures were painted
onto the ceiling blocks in
Egyptian temples, their
wings outspread to protect
the way into the inner sanc-
tum. The most sacred of all
animals to the Egyptians was
the bull Hapi, the reincarna-
tion of the god Ptah. Every
day Hapi was led into the
courtyard of his temple, and
his every movement was
interpreted as foretelling the
future. He was allowed to
live only to a certain age and
was then ritually slaughtered
and buried after a magnificent funeral; huge monolithic
sarcophagi have been found
at Sakkara containing hun-
dreds of mummified bulls.

Discovering Hapi's suc-
cessor occasioned days of
celebration among his fol-
lowers. The lucky calf was
identified by certain mystic
signs: there had to be a
white triangle on its fore-
head, a crescent moon on
its right flank, the image of a
scarab on its tongue and, on
its back, the outline of a vulture with outspread wings.

them was rotten and therefore full of harmful bacteria. Animals that eat food that, to us, smells bad, must in some wise be bad themselves. Most birds have no sense of smell, in itself an oddity; but some New World vultures do have a highly developed sense of smell, and this fact to us seems even odder; why would a bird that can smell putridity seek putridity out and devour it? Vultures are our opposites: we smell rotten meat so that we can avoid it; they smell rotten meat so that they can find it.

From a purely evolutionary standpoint, however, it makes sense to have a taste for food nothing else on the planet except microbes and maggots will touch. The world is full of scavengers, but most of them would rather kill their own food than find it or at least prefer their *trouvailles* to be as fresh as possible and will turn up their noses at carcasses in advanced stages of putrefaction. They don't have the stomach for them. Vultures do. The acid in a vulture's digestive tract is so strong that botulism and cholera bacteria that would wipe out whole villages pass through a vulture like milk through a baby, and studies of vulture excrement show that they actually help control serious outbreaks of anthrax in cattle and swine when they eat infected carcasses; their stomachs destroy the bacteria that cause the diseases. This ability to eat meat that would kill any other carnivores cuts way down on competition and increases the vulture's chances of survival in such fiercely competitive habitats as deserts and tropical forests, as well as in northern boreal environments, where the lineup at a carcass can be twenty or thirty species long. Vultures can afford to wait until the jackals are finished before lying down with the lions.

Vulture Families

THE VULTURE'S ABILITY TO FLOURISH ON PUTRIDITY HAS PROVEN so beneficial that it has risen in nature not once, but twice, resulting in two independent and unrelated strains of vultures. For a long time it was thought that Old World and New World vultures were twin tines of one evolutionary shaft, both families — the Cathartidae (New World) and Accipitridae (Old World) — belonging to the same order, the Falconiformes, or diurnal raptors,

The lammergeier vulture (*Gypaëtus barbatus*) is one of the most common vultures in North Africa and Europe.

birds of prey that do their preying during daylight hours. Other Falconiformes include hawks, kites, ospreys, the secretary bird and the falcons.

In 1873, however, British anatomist A. H. Garrod proposed, on the basis of differences in the thigh muscles of the two groups, that New World vultures were actually more closely related to the order Ciconiiform, which includes storks and herons, than they were to Falconiformes. Other anatomists found that vultures and storks shared other features, such as the intricate pattern of their intestinal coils, that were not shared by hawks. The only thing cathartids and falconids shared, in fact, were hooked beaks, and that hardly made them birds of a feather. In the 1960s, DNA studies confirmed the conjectures of the anatomists: New World vultures are more closely related to storks than they are to Old World vultures; the two vulture assemblages have, in other words, evolved separately, making the similarities between the two families, in the words of one biologist, "one of the more striking examples of evolutionary convergence to be found in the class Aves." Evolutionary convergence occurs when two unrelated families develop strikingly similar traits as a result of living in similar ecological habitats, the theory being that the ability to feed exclusively on already dead animals — an ability that does not require strong talons but is aided by naked heads, flesh-tearing beaks and the means to digest enormous amounts of bacteria without getting sick — was an evolutionary niche waiting to be filled, and the birds that filled it in the New World grew to resemble those that filled it in the Old.

All vultures have powerful, hooked bills designed for gripping and ripping rather than crushing or cutting — the word "vulture" comes from the Latin verb *vellere*, which means "to tear" — which is why they were originally aligned with raptors. But a vulture's feet are adapted for walking and bracing against the ripping force of their beaks rather than for grasping prey and carrying it off to be eaten or stored elsewhere. I have seen hawks, owls and ospreys flying low over meadows and lakes, barely able to clear the ground because of the large payload of fish or rabbit gripped firmly in their strong talons. You'll never see a vulture doing that. Vultures land near a carcass and use their feet to waddle awkwardly around it for a while, making sure that it's dead enough and that nothing else is interested in it before climbing on it preparatory to making that first incision. This is almost always made at one of a carcass's many natural entry points, such as the anus or an eye socket, or else just below one of the scapulae. Vultures may grip the corpse in their beaks and drag it to the shoulder of a highway, but they do not carry off bits of it to consume in trees or nests, as hawks do, and they certainly do not swoop down on living creatures, talons outstretched, brows furrowed, beaks agape in anticipation, as we often see eagles do on flags, coins and tattoos. Nonetheless, both Old and New World vultures have suffered from the supposition that they can do this.

The bearded vulture, for instance, has an undeserved reputation for kidnapping. It was given the name lammergeier ("lamb-vulture") in Germany because of its supposed tendency to make off with newborn lambs and even, in some cases, unattended human babies. These vultures had something of the reputation of wolves in European folklore, though there was always a more alien, otherworldly aura about them. In Greek mythology, it was two bearded vultures, not eagles (as some translations have it), that flew down to tear out Prometheus's liver every day — his punishment for having stolen fire from the gods. A bearded vulture was also blamed for the death of the famous Greek tragedian Aeschylus. The story is that Aeschylus was walking along

AESCHYLVS

a dusty road when a bearded vulture flew overhead carrying a tortoise in its talons; seeing Aeschylus's bald head and mistaking it for a rock, the vulture dropped the turtle in an attempt to crack its shell and cracked the poet's skull instead — to the anachronistic applause of hordes of first-year university English students. Bearded vultures do drop bones on rocks in order to get at the marrow — which is why they were originally called ossifrages — but bones are a lot lighter than tortoises or lambs. Some Old World vultures pick up rocks in their beaks and drop them onto eggs in order to break the eggs, and the anthropologist Jane Goodall, while studying wild canines in Africa, saw a lappet-faced vulture (*Torgos tracheliotus*) attack an eagle in the air while the latter was struggling to carry off a nearly full-grown, live jackal. Vultures are nothing if not opportunistic. But dropping a rock on an egg is a long way from dropping a turtle on a poet, and tussling with an eagle is not the same as carting off newborn babies. Still, myths die hard.

New World vultures have also been accused of hastening the demise of their prey, and here, it must be admitted, there is some justification for the charge. Black vultures (*Coragyps atratus*), for example, have been seen killing piglets in the southern United States, and turkey vultures (*Cathartes aura*) are well known for stealing chicks out of heron nests. In the West, California condors (*Gymnogyps californianus*) have been regularly shot and poisoned by ranchers who believed, on little evidence, that the vultures were killing their calves. Michael Andrews, author of *Flight of the Condor*, was told by a farmer in Peru that Andean condors (*Vultur gryphus*) used to take 90 per cent of the calves during the dry season and that condors would often rush at young goats and lambs to force them over cliffs. But Andrews was unable to confirm the stories, and anyway, no local legend warrants the eradication campaigns that have reduced many New World vulture species to near extinction. Some other, less logical factors must be at work.

Perhaps it is because we know that vultures eat *only* carrion. Even as I write this, a lone turkey vulture is riding the warm air currents above the woods near our cabin, circling back and forth over the treetops, as though in search of something it knows is down here, and I am more disturbed by its presence than I would be by that of, say, a coyote sitting inside the edge of the clearing. I love the forest out here, the ever changing constancy of the natural world, the simple and complex beauty of its greens and greys, the play of light and shadow on the ground and the sound of breeze and birdsong through leaves and grass. The woods here are restful, restorative, full of life, and I do not like to think that Death is as much at home in them as I am. And yet that vulture tells me that something has died in my forest — perhaps the week-old fawn we saw the other day down by the dock, or one of the two loon chicks that rode out onto the lake on their mother's back two days ago. The idea taints the ideal. Do we look up at vultures with the same sense of loss with which we look down into a freshly dug grave? With the knowledge not only that Death occurs, which is a generality, but that a particular death has already occurred?

But What Good Are They?

ALTHOUGH VILIFYING VULTURES BECAUSE OF THEIR UNSAVORY habits or their hideous appearance may be unfair, defending them on the basis of their utility to humans is not the solution. Both approaches raise ethical issues that are being explored by many contemporary biologists, among them Adrian Forsyth, author of *The Nature of Birds* and formerly a neighbour of mine in eastern Ontario. Between my property and Adrian's, where I spent a good deal of time watching him paint numbers on damselflies (family Calopterygidae) or count the offspring of treehoppers (family Membracidae), there was an active turkey vulture roosting site, a large, dead tree in the middle

The
California Condor
in North American
Native
Culture

• FOSSIL REMAINS OF California condors have been found in many archaeological sites in California and Oregon, the most spectacular being at Five Mile Rapids, Oregon. Called a condor cafeteria by researchers, who date the site at 10 000 years before the present, the remains of sixty-three condors were found there; the birds were probably attracted to the site by spawning salmon or by the carcasses of salmon tossed onto the shore by Native fishers.

A site in West Berkeley, California, dating from 3000 years ago, however, yielded an almost complete condor skeleton that had been deliberately buried and arranged in a way resembling human burials from the same site. The burial seems to have been associated with sacrifice: ritual sacrifice of raptors was widely practised. Among the Costanoans, birds of prey were raised from captured chicks and sacrificed at funerals: eagles were sacrificed to the planet Venus, and condors were sacrificed to Mars when Venus was obscured.

In many Native communities, the condor was regarded as a strong source of supernatural power. Shamans received their healing powers from the condor in a dream. Condor body parts were widely used by shamans: condor wing bones were made into tube whistles, used during ceremonial dances, and feathers were used in initiation ceremonies—they were shoved down the throats of prospective shamans to draw blood, which allowed the shaman to become a healer. Condor skins were used by the Pomo and Central Sierra Miwok to make ceremonial suits for the *moloku*, or condor dance.

It is also believed that the Thunderbird of northwest coast mythology was based on the California condor. In the legends of the Tlingit, a people occupying the coast from Alaska to the Queen Charlotte Islands, the condor caused thunder by flapping its wings, and lightning flashed from its red-rimmed eyes. Like the bearded vulture in the Old World, the California condor was feared as an abductor: in Tsimshian legend, the condor flew off with young women and, like a Harpy, caused a great wind to destroy its rivals. Clearly, to Native North Americans, the condor ranked with the raven and eagle as a powerful totemic deity.

Is the Northwest Coast Thunderbird a California condor?
PRINT BY JIM JOHNNY.

Ugliness is in the eye of the beholder; no organism is intrinsically ugly or beautiful useful or harmful, valuable or dispensable.

of a meadow on which five adult vultures would spread their wings to the rising sun as it burned away the chill of the early morning. Adrian and I would regularly pass the roost on our various scurryings along the back road. We would also pass the vultures later in the day, as they lurched grumpily from a freshly killed raccoon cub or gray squirrel that they had dragged to the edge of the ditch. I am doubtless one of those Adrian had in mind when he wrote, "My neighbours find their [vultures'] bald heads and long necks ugly." To Adrian, who is an entomologist, ugliness is in the eye of the beholder; no organism is intrinsically ugly or beautiful, useful or harmful, valuable or dispensable.

"As development continues to encroach upon the natural world," he writes in his chapter on natural inter-relationships, which deals in part with vultures, "naturalists and conservationists are continually called upon to answer the question, But what good is it?" This question has been tiresomely posed since the Age of Reason, when Linnaeus set out to sum up all that was known about the interactions and mutual dependencies among the myriad species he had so painstakingly described and to lay out their

purpose on Earth. Every organism, he says in his essay "The Oeconomy of Nature" (1749), is intricately connected to every other organism, and every-thing, "all these treasures of nature," comprises an almost infinite storehouse of goodies for the sole delight and profit of human beings. Nature's economy is "so artfully contrived, so wonderfully propagated, so providentially supported throughout her three kingdoms," writes Linnaeus, that the world does indeed "seem intended by the Creator for the sake of man. Every thing may be made subservient to his use."

PRECEDING PAGES:
Old World
vultures, such as
these white-backs
in Tanzania,
prefer grassland
habitat. Most New
World vultures,
with their keen
sense of smell, can
forage in the forest
canopy. ART WOLFE

Linnaeus's disciples, particularly those in post-Revolutionary America, felt it their civic duty to rate each species of plant, animal and insect according to its useful-ness to industry and agriculture. They looked at a peri-winkle or a musca fly or a sculpin or a vulture and in each case asked that damnable question: What good is it?

The utilitarian view of nature persisted into the 19th century: although the concept of nature as a source of useful materials was sup-posed to have died out with the Romantics, in fact it merely changed in form. Nature was still useful to human beings, if not economically then as a moral teacher or model for us to follow. Thus Wordsworth in "The Tables Turned":

> One impulse from a vernal wood
> > May teach you more of man,
> Of moral evil and of good,
> > Than all the sages can.

"To ask what this or that is for, with reference to ourselves," wrote American nature writer John Burroughs towards the end of the century, showing that the question was still current then, "and to conclude that some-thing has blundered if it is not of positive use to us is . . . to see and to think like a child." Even so farsighted a writer as George Perkins Marsh, who in his book *Man and Nature* (1873) — widely recognized today as the first work of mod-ern conservationism — warns readers of the dangers inherent in modifying the landscape for their benefit by thoughtless human action, felt obliged to defend various maligned species by pointing out their unsuspected usefulness to the great American economic machine. Sparrows may consume domestic grain, Marsh argued, but in the process they also eat the eggs and larvae of many inju-rious insects. The minute organisms that inhabit the oceans provide the "vast calcareous and silicious deposits" that are so useful to us as chalk and slate. Even those elements of nature that seem useless, in other words, may have hid-den or as yet unknown benefits to humans and should therefore be preserved until those benefits are discovered.

Nature does not benefit from such rationalism, which depends on our knowing something about every species and its relationship to other species and to its environment. Although that sort of knowledge increases every day, sooner or later we will come upon a species for which there is no known benefit to anything but itself. By utilitarian standards, for example, vultures are on shaky ground. It is true that they help keep us from becoming knee-deep in squirrel carcasses. "Vultures," P. A. Taverner noted in 1926 in *Birds of Western Canada*, "are repulsive birds, but as scavengers exceedingly useful, and no valid complaint can be lodged against them." But as Forsyth points out, at least in the eastern deciduous forests of their northern range, "if they did not exist, there are legions of other organisms, such as skunks, opossums, flies, beetles and microbes, that would readily scavenge the same carcasses." Not to mention some relatively "cute" species, such as white admiral butterflies. But Forsyth warns against justifying the preservation of certain animals on the grounds that all species fit into some harmonious natural pattern, that the whole of nature is "bound together by a web of ecological relationships that create a vital living fabric." Many relationships between organisms are antagonistic, and even the harmonious ones are often self-serving and short-lived. The real message of Darwinian evolution is that species exploit one another for their own advantage and that when a relationship ceases to be advantageous to the exploiter it is terminated, often resulting in the extinction of the exploited.

What Forsyth's argument boils down to, then, is that when we are considering whether or not to preserve an endangered species — and, as we shall see, we have had to do just that in the case of the California condor — we must not ask how useful or beneficial that species is to us, or to other species that are beneficial to us, or even how that particular species fits into the complex ecological web of interspecies relationships, which includes us. All we really need to know about a species is that it exists.

New World Vultures

I was much annoyed, and at the same time amused, with the Urubú vultures. The Portuguese call them corvos or crows.

— HENRY WALTER BATES,
The Naturalist on the River Amazons

THE
DIRT ROAD
TO OUR CABIN, LAID OUT
A CENTURY AGO WITHOUT RECOURSE TO
BULLDOZERS OR DYNAMITE, WEAVES AROUND ROCKY

outcroppings and even large trees, climbs up rather than cuts through small hills and makes an extended loop to avoid a swamp that today would have been filled in without a second thought. It is a feat of engineering that acknowledges the primacy of landscape, our own proper place in nature, and even in March, when meltwater from the swamp turns the road into parallel ruts of wheel-sucking gumbo, I pick my way slowly and carefully along it without complaint. And this particular morning in March I was doubly glad I did, because the cautiousness of my approach allowed me to get within a few dozen feet of a turkey vulture before it flapped noisily into the air like a black winding sheet caught in a sudden updraft of wind.

I walked over to see what the vulture had been feeding on. Sometime during the winter, a local trapper had dumped the skinned carcasses of six muskrats into the snow on top of the swamp, and the spring thaw had laid them out neatly on a cushion of thick couch grass, six daily specials in a vulture cafeteria: bright, red-and-white corpses with hairless tails intact and the

Never far from water, this black vulture (*Coragyps atratus*) rests in the Florida Everglades.
ED RECHSLER/PETER ARNOLD, INC.

eyes missing from the grinning skulls. I made a note of the time of day and of the fact that the vulture had been feeding alone and resolved to return the next day earlier to see when the vulture would arrive for breakfast.

Turkey Vultures and Black Vultures

THE TURKEY VULTURE RANGES FROM SOUTHERN CANADA TO South America and is "the chief avian scavenger of the United States," according to vulturologist Winsor Marret Tylor. Sometimes called the turkey buzzard — "buzzard" is actually a British designation for a large hawk, and like the words "robin" and "buffalo," the term has been misapplied in North America — it is a large bird, weighing up to 1.7 kilograms (3.7 pounds) and having a wingspan of nearly 2 metres (6 feet). It is a predominantly black bird with a red, featherless head and neck. The male's head is somewhat wattled, like that of a wild turkey, and as both sexes age their naked necks become more and more wrinkled. Unlike turkeys, though, turkey vultures are most often seen high in the sky, riding the thermals like hawks, hardly ever needing to flap their wings, circling patiently over the landscape until they see or smell something of interest.

You might at first mistake a turkey vulture for a red-tailed hawk or, in the west, a mature golden eagle, but there are several ways to distinguish turkey vultures from other large birds of prey. The bright red head is a dead giveaway, but since a turkey vulture keeps its head drawn closely into its feathered neck ring, or ruff, during flight (to prevent heat loss), this feature is often difficult to detect. Look at the angle of its wings. While soaring, hawks and eagles keep their wings in a more or less straight line, parallel to the ground; vultures, with their larger wing area, hold theirs in a slight V, a formation known as a dihedral. Vultures also waver or wobble on the air currents, tipping back and forth like butterflies; eagles and hawks seem less precariously balanced. They also have pronounced "fingers" at the tips of their wings; these are the primary feathers, which can be manipulated individually for greater flight control.

A black vulture watches for prey from its perch on a cardone cactus in Mexico.

JOHN CANCALOSI/PETER ARNOLD, INC.

Black vultures, also called carrion crows in many parts of their range (true carrion crows, *Corvus corone*, are European members of the crow family) and Jim Crow in the Caribbean, are more numerous than turkey vultures in

Turkey Vulture
Cathartes aura

● Distribution of breeds that are
widely scattered and local to the
north; occasional in winter in
part of this area

● Distribution in all seasons

Distribution of the turkey vulture.
ADAPTED FROM RALPH S. PALMER, ED., HANDBOOK OF
NORTH AMERICAN BIRDS, VOL. 4, *DIURNAL RAPTORS* (PART 1),
NEW HAVEN: YALE UNIVERSITY PRESS, 1988.

most areas where their ranges overlap. They are heavier — around 2 kilograms (4.5 pounds) for adult males — but have shorter wingspans — under 1.5 metres (5 feet) — and have greyish rather than bright red heads (they can be confused with immature turkey vultures in this regard). There is also a touch of white on the undersides of their wings at the base of the primaries that is lacking in turkey vultures. Black vultures, because of their slightly smaller wing area and greater weight, flap more than turkey vultures: their flight pattern tends to be a series of quick wing beats followed by short glides, not unlike that of crows and jays.

The western turkey vulture (*C. aura meridionalis*) is found on both sides of the Rockies, but its range inland is not extensive; it moved into the prairies in the 19th century, attracted by the slaughter of the great bison herds, but the end of the bison wars in the 1890s and the expansion of the coyote into the prairies in the 1920s has pushed the western turkey vulture south again. It is common in California and known as far inland as Montana and has lately been reclaiming some of its lost territory in southern British Columbia (as far north as the Gulf Islands), but not in the numbers recorded near the turn of the century.

The eastern turkey vulture (*C. aura septentrionalis*) is found throughout New England and eastern Canada, from southern Ontario to Venezuela and the Amazon basin in the south. In 1908, its line of northernmost extension was in New Jersey, and the birds would migrate annually from there to their southern wintering grounds in various parts of South America. By the late 1920s, however, turkey vultures had become common, if unwelcome, summer residents in southern New York State, and by 1945, they were occupying most of the area south of the Great Lakes. They moved into Canada a decade later, and are now seen regularly as far north as Ottawa and North Bay. The rapidity of this northern expansion is reflected in spring migration totals at Derby Hill, at the eastern end of Lake Ontario: 60 turkey vultures were spotted there in 1963; 683 in 1977; and 2139 in 1986.

There is a further division of the eastern turkey vulture. David Kirk, a researcher from Scotland who has studied vultures in Venezuela, divides the South American vulture population into two races: migrants and residents. "You can easily tell the difference,"

American Black Vulture
Coragyps atratus

● Approximate overall breeding range; within it, the species is generally absent in all seasons from higher elevations

Distribution of the American black vulture.
ADAPTED FROM RALPH S. PALMER, ED., HANDBOOK OF NORTH AMERICAN BIRDS, VOL. 4, *DIURNAL RAPTORS* (PART 1), NEW HAVEN: YALE UNIVERSITY PRESS, 1988.

he says. "The migrants are bigger and always dominant at a carcass. The residents also have white collars." Kirk noticed that when the migrants return to Venezuela in the fall, the residents retreat to the closed-canopy forests in the interior; as soon as the migrants leave in the spring, the residents move back out into the open savannahs, where the foraging is easier.

The black vulture frequents the same north-south range as the turkey vulture but is a coastal bird, rarely venturing far from the Atlantic shoreline and the margins of rivers and lakes. Its food usually consists of fish, marine reptiles and the young of such birds as herons and gulls. Henry Marston Bates discovered this in the Amazon basin, where black vultures invaded his kitchen during the wet months, but "as the dry season advances, the hosts of Urubús follow the fishermen to the lakes, where they gorge themselves with the offal of the fisheries."

OVERLEAF:
Although awkward when walking on land, black vultures in flight are paragons of grace.
ERWIN AND PEGGY BAUER

David Kirk noticed another difference. Black vultures, he found while live-trapping both black and turkey vultures in Venezuela, are extremely aggressive when handled by researchers. "They pull chunks out of you," he says, "they flap, they stink, they throw up all over you, they do everything all at once. Turkey vultures, on the other hand, are completely passive. When you go up to them they just play possum." In his cage-traps he would sometimes capture twenty vultures at a time: "When I went to take them out the turkey vultures would lie down on the ground and the black vultures would climb up on their bodies to get at me."

Greater and Lesser Yellow-Headed Vultures

LITTLE IS KNOWN ABOUT THE TWO SPECIES OF YELLOW-HEADED vultures found throughout South America: the lesser yellow-headed (*Cathartes burrovianus*) and the greater yellow-headed (*Cathartes melambrotus*). In fact, until 1964 they were considered a single species. And as late as 1994, in a study of greater yellow-heads published in the ornithological journal *Ibis*, Colombian researcher Luis Gomez lamented that even after his exhaustive study, "almost nothing is known about this bird."

Resembling turkey vultures — to which they are closely related — except for a streak of bright yellow at the bill, the lesser yellow-headed vulture is seen more often in open territory than in woodlands. The greater yellow-headed, however, invariably prefers the comfort and security of dense canopy forest and is one of the most conspicuous large birds of the tropical lowlands. Studies by Glasgow ecologist David Houston show that foraging in dense forests makes more sense in the New World than it does in the Old, because Neotropical rain forests contain up to three times more meat per hectare than do most Old World or African forests. Competition is also stronger in the neotropics. As Houston notes, "from a vulture's point of view, finding a carcass is a race against time." Not only do vultures have to beat other scavengers, such as ocelots, jaguars, tayras, armadillos and coatis, to the prize, "but they also have to find the body before insects render it an inedible, maggot-ridden soup."

The greater yellow-headed vulture certainly forages by smell, and the lesser probably does, and both are extraordinarily adept at finding carrion; in

Greater
yellow-headed vultures…
were arguably better at finding food
even than turkey vultures,
ich can sniff out a
dead field mouse
under a manure pile
from a great height.

Gomez's study, conducted with Houston and others in southern Colombia, greater yellow-headed vultures located carcasses buried under piles of leaves 63 per cent of the time, compared with only 5 per cent by their mammalian competitors, and were arguably better at finding food even than turkey vultures, which can sniff out a dead field mouse under a manure pile from a great height. In fact, turkey vultures followed greater yellow-headed vultures to the carcasses, and with king vultures following the turkey vultures, the pecking order at a carrion site, from the mighty king down to the lowly yellow-heads, began to look socially rather complicated.

King Vultures

IN 1774, THE INTREPID NATURALIST WILLIAM Bartram walked the St. John's River, in Florida, and made lengthy observations of the birds he saw there. "There are two species of vultures in these regions, I think not mentioned in history," he wrote in his *Travels*, published in 1791:

the first we shall describe as a beautiful bird, near the size of a turkey buzzard, but his wings are much shorter and consequently he falls greatly below that admirable bird in sail. .... The bill is long and straight almost to the point, when it is hooked or bent suddenly down and sharp; the head and neck bare of feathers nearly down to the stomach, when the feathers begin to cover up the skin, and soon become long and of a soft texture, forming a ruff or tippet, in which the bird by contracting his neck can hide that as well as his head; the bare skin on the neck appears loose and wrinkled, and is of a deep bright yellow

The King Vulture in Mayan Legend

• THE KING VULTURE'S scientific name, *Sarcorhamphus papa*, translates as "the Pope's fleshy beak," a reference to the lump of bright orange skin that sits atop its orange beak. The bird's common name, however, goes back much farther in time than the Spanish conquest of South America, as a recent archaeological site in Belize has made dramatically clear.

In the pre-Columbian city of La Milpa, in Belize, archaeologists Norman Hammond and Gair Tourtellot discovered a Mayan royal tomb >>>

>>> dating from A.D. 450, containing the remains of a ruler known as Bird Jaguar. The king's body was adorned with ear ornaments and a necklace of totemic heads carved in light green jade; it also bore a large pendant of a vulture's head, carved from jade that probably originated in Guatemala. It is the head of a king vulture and, says Hammond, is "a unique piece of Maya lapidary art."

In Mayan legend, human beings descended from the jaguar, and the vulture was the messenger who mediated between humans and the gods. Personified as a lord or king, "he was the conduit to the gods and the otherworld in his lifetime," Hammond told a conference on Maya Kings and Warfare at the British Museum in 1996, and was "deified and venerated as an ancestor and god after his death."

colour, intermixed with coral red; the hinder part of the neck is nearly covered with short, stiff hair; and the skin of this part of the neck is of a dun-purple colour, gradually becoming red as it approaches the yellow of the sides and fore part. The crown of the head is red; there are lobed lappets of a reddish orange colour, which lie on the base of the upper mandible. But what is singular, a large portion of the stomach hangs down on the breast of the bird, in the likeness of a sack or half wallet, and seems to be a duplicature of the craw, which is naked and of a reddish flesh colour; this is partly concealed by the feathers of the breast, unless when it is loaded with food . . . , and then it appears prominent. The plumage of the bird is generally white or cream colour, except the quill-feathers of the wings and two or three rows of the coverts, which are of a beautiful dark brown; the tail, which is large and white, is tipped with this dark brown or black; the legs and feet of a clear white; the eye is encircled with a gold coloured iris; the pupil black.

Bartram called this peculiar bird the painted vulture, or *Vultur sacra*, and for many years its identity remained a complete ornithological mystery; no one else saw it. John Cassin, the curator of the Academy of Natural Sciences in Philadelphia, wrote in 1853 that "there is no more inviting nor more singular problem in North American ornithology" than the identification of the bird described by Bartram. Many ornithologists thought that *Vultur sacra* was the king vulture (*Sarcorhamphus papa*), but no king vultures had been found in Florida.

The king vulture is now exclusively a tropical bird, ranging from central Mexico to northern Argentina. The most magnificently coloured vulture in the world, it strongly resembles Bartram's description: the red-crowned head and orange lappets; the naked head and neck ending, at the shoulders, in a soft ruff; the white or cream-coloured plumage; the dark brown wing feathers. Only in the matter of the troublesome tail feathers do the two birds differ: the king vulture has black tail feathers, while those described by Bartram were white tipped with dark brown or black. The problem was finally settled by Francis Harper in 1936: the king vulture does have a black tail, but it also has short, white under-tail coverts, visible when the tail is spread during flight, that may appear, from a distance and before the advent of binoculars, to be part of the larger tail feathers. Bartram's reputation was restored, but Harper's solution raised another question (as do most solutions to scientific queries): what drove the king vulture out of Florida?

A robust bird — at 81 centimetres (32 inches) in length and with a wingspan of almost 2 metres (6.5 feet), it is the largest of the New World vultures — even within its present range, it was reported to be "rare in most localities" as early as 1924; its optimum population density is about 1 per 1.25 square kilometres (or 2 per square mile), meaning that it doesn't take many deaths to render it a rare bird. King vultures do not do well in cold, and Florida has been known to have prolonged cold spells: the frost of 1835 is said to be responsible for the eradication of the royal palm in northern Florida and could have had the same effect on the king vulture. The young remain in the nest for about four months and then maintain contact with the parent birds for a long time; a juvenile male king vulture does not reach sexual maturity until it is four and a half years old; a female somewhat sooner. All of which makes the king vulture a dubious candidate for northern expansion.

The Love Season

VULTURES HAVE BEEN ON THE DECLINE IN NORTH AND SOUTH America since the arrival of European settlers. Though not officially endangered, the turkey vulture is on the Audubon Society's Blue List, which means it is being closely monitored. The decline in most species is largely due to habitat loss, but is also partly a consequence of the birds' size and breeding habits. Turkey vultures are large birds, and large birds usually lay large eggs in small clutches and incubate them for a longer time, and their young take

OVERLEAF: A young turkey vulture in Texas dries its wing feathers in the morning sun before leaving the roost.
TOM AND PAT LEESON

longer to fledge and reach independence than, say, young robins or sparrows. And like the young of most large species, young vultures tend to hang around the family long after they have fledged, begging scraps of food from their parents for up to six months. While none of this actually explains their decline, all of it mitigates against their recovery.

John James Audubon, writing in 1840, describes the courtship ritual of the black vulture with a certain degree of fascination:

> At the commencement of the love season, which is about the beginning of February, the gesticulations and parade of the males are extremely ludicrous. They first strut somewhat in the manner of the Turkey Cock, then open their wings, and, as they approach the female, lower their head, its wrinkled skin becoming loosened, so as entirely to cover the bill, and emit a puffing sound, which is by no means musical. When these actions have been repeated five or six times, and the conjugal compact sealed, the "happy pair" fly off and remain together until their young come abroad.

This ground display is preceded by five or ten minutes of communal frenzied wheeling and chasing in the air, the males flying centimetres behind the females, before a pair plunges to the ground to commence its strange dance. For turkey vultures, the conjugal compact is permanent; they mate for life. Divorce is not uncommon in black vultures.

For all vultures, the word "nest" is always a verb, never a noun. Vultures nest, but they do not make nests. They do not cushion their eggs while brooding, nor do they so much as scratch out a hollow or enlarge a cavity for the greater comfort or security of the egg; they simply lay the eggs on the bare ground more or less as they find it. The following account, recorded by an egg collector named Walter Hoxie, of a visit to Buzzard Island off the coast of South Carolina in 1886, is typical:

> Perhaps a dozen or twenty pairs [of vultures] breed here regularly, the most of them being the Black species, though one or two pairs of the Turkey Buzzards may be observed nearly every year. . . . Here,

under a dense growth of yucca, I have taken nineteen eggs in one afternoon, and seen at the same time five or six pairs of newly hatched young. There is never the slightest attempt at forming a nest, or even excavating a hollow. The eggs are laid far in under the intertwining stems of the yucca, and in the semi-shadows are quite hard to be seen.

Black and turkey vultures once preferred to nest in bottomland hardwood forests and thickets, close to water, but now, as large hardwood trees become increasingly scarce, vultures favour rocky cliffs or talus slopes, especially if there are caves or other dark recesses, such as those provided by fallen slabs of rock, to provide a modicum of shelter. Nests are still found in hollow trees and under fallen logs, when available, and turkey vultures have even been found nesting in abandoned buildings. An effort is made to place the eggs in some sort of shade so that they do not become addled while the parents are off eating carrion, but this is fairly rudimentary parenting. Egg collectors of a more innocent era discovered that if they stole the eggs from a black vulture nest, the vulture would lay a second clutch within the next three weeks — a phenomenon known to biologists as double-clutching — but not in the same nest: a second nest is chosen a short distance from the first. This phenomenon bespeaks a certain degree of care in selecting nest sites, but even pigeons, which lay their eggs any old place as long as it is near the edge of a cliff, are known to kick a few twigs or pebbles into a heap and then defecate on it to keep it together before ovipositing directly on top of the spindly mess. Vultures place more trust in luck than they do in nest building. They do not seem to compensate for their carelessness by being copious egg producers: they lay usually two eggs, sometimes only one, almost never three, every second year.

There is no evidence of double-clutching among turkey vultures, perhaps because there is no time; black vultures lay their eggs two weeks earlier than turkey vultures at the same latitude. In the lower latitudes (below 30 degrees north), black vulture eggs are laid in February or early March; in higher latitudes (30 to 45 degrees north), the eggs are laid in April. Although in captivity black vultures have no trouble breeding at higher latitudes, their failure to expand into northern regions probably has to do with their feeding strategies.

Turkey vultures can more easily find small food items by smell — black vultures, which have no sense of smell, need a large and consistent source of food.

Eggs, Eggs, Eggs

TURKEY VULTURE EGGS ARE LARGISH, AVERAGING 71 MILLIMETRES by 48 millimetres (3 inches by 2 inches), about the size of a goose's egg but smaller than an eagle's. In shape they are elliptical or elongate-ovate, ensuring that if the eggs roll, they roll around in circles rather than straight over a cliff edge. Black vulture eggs are slightly smaller. It used to be thought that of two eggs in a clutch, one would hatch a male chick and the other a female and that

the egg containing the male was slightly more elliptical than elongate, but science has not yet confirmed this supposition. The eggs of both species are off-white, with smooth, finely granulated shells that show little or no gloss and are decorated with random brown or liver-coloured splotches that may act as a kind of camouflage in dappled light.

The eggs, and the chicks that hatch from them, are thus quite vulnerable to predation from such mammals as mongeese (especially in Jamaica), skunks, foxes, raccoons, opossums and humans, as well as from other birds, such as crows and ravens. And in nests on talus slopes or on low ground near water, flooding from spring runoff is often a problem.

The eggs are incubated by both parents, at twenty-four-hour intervals, for periods varying from twenty-eight to forty-one days, depending on the climate and the latitude. In their southern range, the average is around thirty-one days, but farther north the longer periods are more usual. The reason is probably that in the north, where winters are longer and trees are smaller,

ABOVE:
Turkey vultures lay one or two mottled eggs on the bare ground but fiercely protect them from predators.

ROB SIMPSON/VALAN

the vultures tend to nest more often in caves and on talus slopes, which are colder even than the surrounding air. It has been noted that vultures tend to choose cliff faces that face south, and the rocks do tend to hold the heat, but a severe winter and a late spring can be hard on all early-breeding birds, especially those that do not make nests.

King vultures, which are between turkey vultures and the condors in size, generally lay only one egg around the end of November, the end of the rainy season. The adults incubate the eggs for a much longer period than smaller vultures do — up to fifty-six days.

Nasty Nestlings

WHEN YOUNG VULTURES HATCH, THEY ARE A FLUFFY, DOWNY white and weigh only about 50 grams (2 ounces). Between hatchling and adult, they thus multiply their weight by a factor of 30 — the same ratio as for humans, except that vultures do it in about eighty-one days, whereas we take eighteen years. They achieve half this remarkable gain in the first twenty-one days. The chicks are fed by the parent birds, which swallow much more food than they can digest, bring back the undigested portion in their crops and regurgitate it for the young. Figures for turkey and black vultures are not available, but studies of the energy requirements of South Africa's Cape vultures (*Gyps coprotheres*) show that nestlings require about 800 grams (28 ounces) of meat per day, whereas adults need only about 417 grams (15 ounces); adult Cape vultures' stomachs are large enough to hold 1500 grams (3.3 pounds) of food — the amount of meat left, say, on a two-month-old hyena that has been hit by an eighteen-wheel tractor-trailer — the extra space holds food for the children.

Brooding is also shared by both sexes, at least for the first five days after hatching, at which time the hatchlings achieve thermal independence and can be left for short periods while the parents forage. After two weeks, the adults make only infrequent feeding visits to their young. Each time they do, they land near the nest and, in case anyone is watching, spend the next fifteen minutes or so looking very nonchalant, preening their feathers, hopping around in different directions; no doubt, if they had lips, they would whistle. Then they hop suddenly and clumsily into the nest and spend exactly one minute feeding the chicks. This charade takes place three times a day and will go on until the chicks leave the nest.

An observer from Winnipeg in the 1930s described the scene at the nest when an adult vulture arrived at dinnertime: "Both young rushed toward the female parent with wide-spread wings. The first to reach her thrust its bill well into the parent's gullet, the old bird stretching out low over the rock to facilitate the exchange of regurgitated food. The feeding process was carried on so vigorously that it resembled a tussle, both birds swaying their heads up and down and from side to side and balancing themselves by raising their wings."

Disturbing a vulture nest with young vultures in it is not a good idea. Although the parents usually retreat to the nearest tree, the chicks are prone to retaliate. First, the nestlings will lower their heads and hiss at you like rattlesnakes, holding their wings out on both sides, wrists bent down, tips touching ground, and charge at you like a pair of hellcats spitting fire. It is all bluff, of course, and when it doesn't work, they will hide in a corner of the nest and glare at you. If further pressed, they will disgorge the unlovely contents of their stomachs and craws onto your hands. Vultures also have a habit of excreting on their own legs, to help them cool off when excited, and being handled gets them excited. While on Buzzard Island in 1886, Walter Hoxie recalled an incident involving his companion, F, who was trying to steal black vulture eggs and surprised a well-grown pair of chicks. F "was so well wedged in among the yucca stems," chuckles Hoxie, "that he could neither make his escape nor defend himself. When he did get out, he was streaming with filth, excrement and blood, and his language was simply awful."

Perhaps, though, vultures can distinguish between intruders intent on robbing a nest and those making purely scientific observations, for another observer, Laurie A. McHargue, of the Smithsonian Tropical Research Institute, who regularly examined a pair of nestlings in Panama in 1978, weighing and photographing them every three days for twelve weeks, reports that "the nestlings never regurgitated when handled." Similarly, Canadian naturalist R. D. Lawrence, upon discovering a turkey vulture nest in Ontario and crawling in for a closer look, picked up a chick (which he describes as "the ugliest creature on Earth") and even stroked the wing feathers of the adult, without incurring any sort of tangible wrath.

The chicks begin to leave the nest at six weeks of age, and for the next month they spend 80 per cent of their daylight hours outside, perching on low branches, hopping about and flapping their increasingly feathered wings in mock flight. They nibble and tug at twigs, no doubt practising for future carcass work. They also nibble and tug at each other, antics that researchers view as training for later behaviour between adults, especially between mating pairs.

The nest is abandoned in most latitudes sometime between late August and mid-September. By this time, the chicks' plumage is well developed, although there is still a lot of white in it. I once saw a fledgling turkey vulture hopping about on a forest floor, and it was such a mottled white and black that I thought at first it was a domestic chicken, until I saw that it was *eating* a domestic chicken. The young adult attempts short flights first, from one easily reached perch to another, but after a week it is flying as well as, and generally with, its parents. As with humans, independence in the juvenile does not relieve the adults of their parental responsibilities; the adults continue to bring food to the young vultures, or at least lead them to where food can be found, for up to six months after the juveniles are perfectly capable of finding it for themselves. The reason for this assistance is clear: when you raise only one or two offspring every two years, you want to make sure they survive. The 19th-century adage that nature is careless of individuals but careful of species is only partly true; it is by looking after individuals that the species is taken care of.

Roosting and Feeding

AFTER NESTING AND CHICK REARING, THE MOST IMPORTANT adult activity for many birds, including vultures, is communal roosting, the strategy of birds to gather together in large groups to spend the night. Black vultures congregate every day, late in the afternoon, and fill several trees with their spectral shapes; turkey vultures roost in smaller numbers, sometimes only three or four, and sometimes mixed in with the larger black vulture roosts.

Black Vulture

Coragyps atratus
Pablo Neruda

• The vulture opened its Parish,
endorsed its black habits,
flew about in search of sinners,
diminutive crimes, robberies,
lamentable cattle thefts,
inspecting everything from above:
fields, homes, dogs, sand,
it sees everything without looking,
flies outstretched, opening
its priestly garb to the sun.

The vulture, God's spy,
does not smile at springtime:
it circles round and round, measuring heaven,
solemnly settles on the ground,
and folds up like an umbrella.

Roosting areas are more or less permanent and have nothing to do with the location of nesting areas or even feeding sites. Black vultures will sometimes roost near a large carcass, but only until that carcass is gone, at which time they'll return to their regular roost.

The purpose of roosting is a matter of some conjecture. Migrating monarch butterflies, for example, roost probably to conserve heat during the night; rock doves and migrating semipalmated sandpipers may roost for safety, as a strategy to confuse predators. Roosting in vultures seems to have more to do with sharing various kinds of knowledge. Roosts, in other words, may act as information centres where successful birds — those who are good at finding food — pass on information to less successful birds of the same family or clan. The successful foragers leave the roost early in the morning with a specific goal in mind — the carcass they found the previous day — and the less successful foragers simply follow them to the carcass.

Turkey vultures are more territorial than black vultures or yellow-headed vultures. David Kirk says that he has seen as many as a hundred black vultures feeding contentedly together on a single capybara carcass weighing less than 4 kilograms (9 pounds), whereas turkey vultures feed one at a time, dominant male first, while the others stand off to one side, in the manner of beta wolves and coyotes, shuffling their feet and making light conversation until it is their turn to gorge. As Kirk points out, turkey vultures are hierarchical feeders that need to domi-

Old World vultures (PAGE 57) and New World vultures (PAGE 59) appear to be related, but they have merely evolved along parallel lines in response to similar environments.
ART WOLFE

Black vultures congregate every day late in the afternoon, and fill several trees with their spectral shap

PRECEDING PAGES:
Vulture stomachs
contain strong
acids, enabling
them to feed
on carcasses, such
as this giraffe,
that predators
leave behind.
DOUGLAS T.
CHEESEMAN, JR./PETER
ARNOLD, INC.

nate a carcass, and it is easier to defend a smaller carcass than a large one. "A cow carcass," he says, "just has too many entry points, and it would take a great deal of energy for a turkey vulture to defend it against a horde of black vultures." Turkey vultures, in other words, may have evolved to fill the small-carcass niche so that they wouldn't have to share their food with anybody.

This difference between black and turkey vultures is also reflected in the way the two species roost. While studying black vultures in North Carolina, Patricia Parker Rabenold, a vulture researcher at Ohio State University, has found that a distinct roosting, flight and feeding pattern emerges in the vultures' daily comings and goings. The vultures eat primarily during the morning hours and spend the warm afternoons circling on the thermals in search of the next day's meal. When they have found a likely carcass, they swoop down to investigate it but do not eat from it right away; instead, they return to the communal roosting site, usually in the late afternoon, and sleep overnight. In the morning, the successful foragers will leave the roost early in the morning, before the air has really warmed up, and fly directly to the carcass found the previous afternoon. These birds will be followed by several others who were unsuccessful in finding a carcass, leading Rabenold to surmise that the value, if not the purpose, of communal roosting is to share vital knowledge with other vultures, possibly family members, so that food resources will be shared out among the roost. "Vultures have to rely on widely dispersed, unpredictable food supply," Rabenold writes; "therefore cooperation increases success." In other words, the more vultures out there scouting out food sources over a wide area, the more likely it is that everyone will get something to eat, provided the information is shared.

A different pattern emerges among turkey vultures. Turkey vultures usually leave the roost to search for food individually, about two hours after sunrise. Black vultures straggle out about an hour later, always in groups. Sometimes later groups of black vultures will follow the early group and join in the communal feast immediately upon arrival. When a turkey vulture joins another turkey vulture already feeding, however, it waits its turn. But both black and

Turkey vultures
(Cathartes aura)
roost in small
family groups in
forested areas
from Canada
to South America.
MICHAEL EVAN SEWELL

turkey vultures wheel in the air above a carcass for a time before descending, an activity, Rabenold points out, that is unnecessary unless it is designed to tell other vultures of their find.

Why would a vulture want to tell other vultures where its food is located? With black vultures, which prefer larger carcasses, it may be because they need cooperative effort to feed; two or more birds can pull the skin off a dead donkey more efficiently than one. Turkey vultures don't need help to disembowel a chipmunk. Rabenold suspects that turkey vultures may return to the roost to recruit particular individuals — family members, or their own young. Sexually immature turkey vultures remain in contact with their parents for several years, and it is possible that parents intentionally train them in the fine art of finding food during that time, again as a means of increasing the likelihood that their own genetic material will survive.

Even so, vulture populations in North and South America, never high to begin with, are continuing to decline in many parts of their range. Loss of nesting habitat and conflict with human beings, combined with a slow reproductive rate, have placed these magnificent birds in jeopardy. As we shall see in the next chapter, the condor branch of the vulture family is hovering on the very brink of extinction. There may be little we can or should do to correct natural declines, but declines caused by human intervention can and should be reversed. It is important for us to realize that a threat to any member of the natural community is a threat to us all.

3

As for birds, there are some so small they
are taken for bees or butter-flies; And others
in call'd Condores, so vastly big that
they'll kill a Calf and devour a great Part of it.
— PASCOE THOMAS,
Commodore Anson's Voyage

El Condor Pasa

PERHAPS BECAUSE OF ITS NAME, THE CALIFORNIA

CONDOR (*GYMNOGYPS CALIFORNIANUS*)

IS CONSIDERED TO BE A WESTERN BIRD, AND INDEED within living memory its range extended from lower California to southern British Columbia. But fossil evidence from excavations of Pleistocene sites as far away as Florida, southern Mexico and upper New York State show that the California condor and its earlier, even larger ancestors once ranged over all of North and Central America. The California condor is a kind of living fossil: virtually unchanged since the Pleistocene, it has slowly been declining in number and range ever since. What is seen today as a recent shrinkage of its population and territory may therefore be only an acceleration of a gradual process that has been going on for nearly 2 million years.

The California condor is a large vulture: an adult weighs more than 9 kilograms (20 pounds) and has a wingspan of nearly 3 metres (10 feet). Some of the earlier vulturids, however, were even larger. Consider, for example, the extinct vultures known as the teratornids. *Teratornis merriami* weighed up to 14.5 kilograms (32 pounds) and had a 3.6-metre (12-foot) wingspan, and was the largest bird ever to take to the air.

Large birds tend to specialize in large prey animals and therefore have a harder time making a living than smaller birds do. The story of the decline of the California condor is in part the story of the loss of many of the large mammals that roamed throughout North America. This decline began during the last Ice Age, which tended to favour smaller animals and wipe out such large beasts as the stag-

The wild California condor (*Gymnogyps californianus*) population dwindled to three birds before a captive breeding program rescued the species from extinction in 1987.

ERWIN AND PEGGY BAUER

moose, the American mastodon, the woolly mammoth, the ground sloth and the giant beaver, all of which became extinct eleven thousand to nine thousand years ago. The disappearance of their principal food source precipitated the decline of the California condor.

The arrival of Europeans in North America hastened the process begun by global climate change, as they set about eliminating most of the large species they found here, killing the herbivores outright and slowly driving the carnivores west and north: wolves, wolverines, grizzly bears and cougars once held the same range across North America as the California condor but now too are predominantly western animals.

The story of the California condor is therefore not an isolated one of the decline and fall of a single species but is rather an example of the effects of two very powerful ecological forces, both of which are still in operation: dramatic climate change and human encroachment on wilderness territory. Both forces have a similar impact — habitat loss — a double whammy that spells doom to a great many species.

The Decline of the California Condor

THE CALIFORNIA CONDOR HAS FEW BASIC REQUIREMENTS FOR survival, but they are rigid. Its single egg, like those of all vulture species, is laid every second year, usually on bare ground in the merest pretense of a nest. The bird frequents high, mountainous regions where there are more mountain sheep and deer than people. It requires large, isolated areas — a single adult condor cruises over 250 square kilometres (100 square miles) a day in search of carrion and, at least during nesting season, is extremely wary of humans. The sound of an approaching researcher or even a passing airplane will cause it to abandon its nest for hours, sometimes long enough for the single egg to cool

ABOVE:
The California condor has a larger wingspan than any other North American Bird.
MIKE WALLACE/LOS ANGELES ZOO

or the newly hatched chick to starve. Vast, uninhabited territories and undis-turbed solitude, however, are exactly the conditions that disappear as human settlement extends into wilderness territory. The California condor has been called the canary in the mine shaft for assessing the ecological health of the West; its decline is a symptom that something has gone wrong with the wilder-ness. As ecologist David Brower puts it, "When the vultures watching your society begin to drop dead, it's time to pause and wonder."

No one knows how many condors rode the Pacific coast thermals in pre-historic times, but it is known that the bird was important to West Coast natives as long ago as 2200 years before the present and was known from southern Alaska to northern Mexico, and from the Pacific coast to Florida.

By the middle of the 19th century, however, the California condor had already begun to decline in number and shrink in range. By the late 1930s, con-dor researcher Carl Koford esti-mated that only about sixty con-dors remained in the wild, most of them within a day's drive of Los Angeles. The bird was placed on the U.S. federal Endangered Species list in 1967 — six years before the Endangered Species Act passed into law — becoming the flagship of the movement to save threatened and endangered species. Despite the attention, however, the condor continued to decline. A 1965 survey found only forty condors left, and Margaret Millar — wife of mys-tery writer Ross Macdonald and a respected amateur ornithologist whose book *The Birds and Beasts Were There* (1967) is a wonderful account of birding in California

Distribution of the California condor.
ADAPTED FROM RALPH S. PALMER, ED., HANDBOOK OF NORTH AMERICAN BIRDS, VOL. 4, *DIURNAL RAPTORS* (PART 1), NEW HAVEN: YALE UNIVERSITY PRESS, 1988.

California Condor
Gymnogyps Californianus

Putative past distribution, extrapolated from Pleistocene and prehistoric site records

Additional location, about 10 500 years ago

Recent (1989) total range, occupied by three birds

— pointed out that there were three times as many stuffed California condors in the world's museums than there were live ones in California. "I think we can safely assume," she wrote, "that very few of them died of heart attacks."

The annual survey of condors initiated in 1965 was kept up until 1981 and showed that condor numbers were falling steadily at the rate of two to four birds per year. The California condor is not a prolific breeder by any standards; like other large New World vultures, it lays only one egg every two years, and its young take six years to reach sexual maturity. Individual condors can live to the age of sixty, but most of them don't, partly for natural reasons and partly because we continue to invade and destroy their habitat in ways we may already have lost the ability to control.

By 1981, only nineteen condors were left in the wild, most of them in the 21 500 hectares (53 000 acres) that then made up the Los Padres National Forest in southern California's Central Valley. Three years later, the figure dropped to fifteen. Total extinction of the California condor was predicted for sometime between 1990 and 2000, depending on how you plotted the decline, and even that was considered by some to be optimistic. "Regardless of whose population estimates one prefers," concluded a 1983 report, "the California condor appears to be heading rapidly towards extinction."

A radio tag affixed to the wing of an adult male condor in the fall of 1982 led U.S. Fish and Wildlife biologist Noel Snyder, who was working with the government's official Condor Recovery Team, to conclude that the birds were feeding exclusively on two types of carrion: piles of deer entrails left by hunters, and dead calves on cattle ranges. In other words, condors were relying completely on food made available to them by human activities. In a sense, then, the condor was no longer a wild bird but was dependent for its subsistence on human beings. This was an ironic and worrisome state of affairs. Ironic because human activities, long known to be responsible for the condor's drastic decline, now appeared to be its sole means of support. And worrisome because it raised what turned out to be a highly controversial question: if humans were responsible for the condor's tailspin towards extinction, were we not therefore responsible for its protection?

Although few argued against protecting the condor, how best to go about it was a highly charged question, and the stances taken by various groups more

The California condor has been called the canary in the mine shaft for assessing the ecological health of the West.

or less typify the problems inherent in any venture into wildlife management. One of the first ideas put forward was to institute an urgent captive breeding program: send biologists out into condor country, capture a breeding stock from among the last few wild condors, put them in a zoo and release the eventual chicks back into the wild.

This idea was almost instantly opposed by environmentalists, many of whom advocated leaving the condors alone and concentrating on habitat rehabilitation. Educate hunters and ranchers to stop poisoning carcasses with strychnine and Compound 1080 to kill coyotes, stop the spraying of DDT and organochlorines, they said, and the condor population will bounce back. Two early proponents of this approach were the brothers Ian and Eben McMillan, who lived on a ranch in southern California, where, in the 1970s, the California condor seemed to be making its last stand against extinction. The McMillan brothers were among the first to sound the condor alarm. Eben McMillan spoke eloquently and passionately at Audubon Society meetings for the preservation of condors and condor habitat. Ian McMillan's book, *Man and the California Condor*, is a withering account of our desecration of Western habitat.

Carl Koford opposed captive breeding on ethical grounds. "A condor in a cage," Koford wrote in a monograph published by the Audubon Society shortly before his death in 1979, "is uninspiring, pitiful, and ugly to one who has seen them soaring over the mountains." But he also firmly believed captive breeding wouldn't work: he didn't think that captive-raised birds would survive when released into the wild, and he worried that instituting a captive breeding program would be seen as a quick fix, removing public attention from the important goals of habitat protection and legislation prohibiting the hunting and poisoning of condors. "If we cannot preserve condors in the wild through understanding their environmental relations," Koford wrote, "we have already lost the battle and may be no more successful in preserving mankind."

The National Audubon Society, Sierra Club and Friends of the Earth all advocated leaving the California condor alone and concentrating on environmental improvement. David Brower even maintained that the condor should always "live free" and be allowed to "die with dignity," in essence, that the species should be permitted to run its natural course to extinction, which seems to have begun ten thousand years ago.

But there were those who pointed out that the condor's present accelerated decline was anything but natural, that death by DDT or Compound 1080 or strychnine is not dignified, and that we have a moral obligation to preserve any threatened or endangered species if it is in our power to do so. That was the position ultimately taken by the Condor Recovery Team, which established the Condor Research Center in Ventura, California, and was made up of scientists from various federal, state and private organizations, including the Fish and Wildlife Service and the California Fish and Game Commission, under the auspices of the Department of the Interior. In the recovery team's view, agonizing over habitat loss and the ethics or aesthetics of captivity was a luxury that came second to a clear and obvious fact: unless something drastic was done immediately, the world would be minus one more species of large scavenger and all questions of habitat and ethics would become academic.

In 1982, the team removed the first egg from the nest of a wild California condor. In fact, they removed two: one from a nest in Ventura County and another from the nest of a particularly fertile mating pair in Santa Barbara County. The eggs were placed in incubators in the San Diego Zoo; later that summer, when the eggs were successfully hatched, the chicks were transferred to the zoo's Wild Animal Park. The team did not stop at egg removal; in August of that year, Snyder and Phil Ensley of the San Diego Zoo also took the first wild-hatched chick from the Ventura County nest and placed it in the Wild Animal Park. The first giant step towards captive breeding had been taken.

The Condor Recovery Team's strategy was based on new knowledge of condor behaviour obtained by the Condor Research Center. The egg-removal program was possible because the team was now certain that the California condor was able to "double-clutch," that is, to lay a second, replacement egg if the first one was lost. Until 1981, it was thought that California condors did not double-clutch. It was known that Andean condors and turkey vultures double-clutched, but Koford, who knew more about California condors than anyone, had by 1979 found no evidence that the California condor laid replacement eggs and firmly stated that it did not. In 1981, however, Snyder and his colleagues began to keep watch on the two fertile wild condors in Santa Barbara County, known as the Santa Barbara pair. The pair began incubating an egg on February 14, 1982, but about two weeks into the incubation

The Decline of
Old World
Vultures

• THE MAJOR SPECIES of vultures in Europe—the Egyptian, the bearded, the griffon and the black or cinereous vultures—have suffered serious declines in population since the 1950s and are all but extinct in many parts of the continent. One study estimated that vulture populations in Europe are about 1 per cent of what they were 150 years ago. The bearded vulture, for example, once the most common vulture in Europe, is now reduced to about 80 pairs in total, and most of those are found in Spain (20 pairs), the French Pyrénées (10 pairs) and Greece (35 pairs).

The cinereous vulture, also a once common European species, is similarly afflicted. Although a population count in Spain in 1974 yielded 206 pairs, numbers have been declining steadily ever since: a single colony dropped from 45 pairs in 1965 to 18 pairs in the mid-1970s. A shy bird of the lowland pine forest, the cinereous vulture is easily disturbed by human encroachment. In Greece, the last stronghold of the species in eastern Europe, there are fewer than 15 mating pairs, although recent legislation and efforts by the World Wildlife Fund have helped to stabilize the decline.

Reasons for these declines are not difficult to find. The longest-standing cause has been reduction in food supplies, as farming practices in Europe shifted from nomadic flocks of sheep and goats to more concentrated types of agriculture, in which domestic stock is kept in protected compounds. Hunting has also declined in Europe as wild animals have disappeared, and carcasses left behind by hunters were a major source of food for vultures. Habitat loss, especially of nesting sites, is also an important factor. The spread of civilization into hitherto inaccessible regions, in the form of hydro dams, power lines and roads, has disturbed many of the areas formerly the exclusive domain of the vulture.

Perhaps the most serious and long-term threat to vulture populations, however, has been the introduction of a wide variety of poisons into the food chain. In the 1950s—the decade that marked the beginning of vulture decline—the practice of placing strychnine in animal carcasses to control foxes, wolves and jackals became common, and vultures, feeding on the poisoned remains of these predators, were in turn poisoned by them. In Israel, researchers trace the decline of the Egyptian vulture to "exaggerated applications" of thallium sulfate to control an infestation of field mice in 1950. Once the most common vulture in Israel, the Egyptian vulture had been reduced to a mere 58 pairs by 1980.

period, they got into a domestic squabble over whose turn it was to sit on the egg, and, with the recovery team watching helplessly through field glasses from a distance, the egg went hurtling over the cliff. "Forty days later," reported a jubilant Snyder, "the female laid a second egg in another cave about a hundred metres distant on the same cliff." The team, now armed with a priori evidence that condors laid replacement eggs, obtained permission from the Fish and Wildlife Service (FWS) and the California Fish and Game Commission to begin a program of deliberate egg removal. In 1983, three eggs were taken from wild condor nests, and in 1984, four more. "Three of the four pairs from which eggs were taken laid replacements," says Snyder; "two pairs even laid three eggs within single breeding seasons." In other words, the team now had a method of doubling or even tripling the reproductive rate of wild California condors.

The team's second strategy — taking live chicks from wild condor nests and raising them in San Diego's Wild Animal Park — was similarly based on recently improved knowledge of condor behaviour. Koford had hypothesized that the task of raising chicks to maturity consumed so much energy that condors could only afford to do it once every two years, and that the resulting slow reproduction rate was the principal cause of its decline. One chick every two years was simply not enough to keep the species going, especially — as later ecologists pointed out — when egg and chick mortality was increasing because of manufactured contaminants such as DDT and its metabolite, DDE. As with the bald eagle and the peregrine falcon, high levels of DDE in the birds' diets caused them to lay eggs with shells too thin to support their own weight; the eggs broke from the impact of being laid.

Furthermore, the egg-removal program exacerbated the wild condor's chick-rearing problems: if the first egg were taken, and, a month later, the pair laid a replacement clutch, the second chick would hatch very late in the fall and would still be dependent on its parents for support the following spring, when egg-laying time came around again. Having a dependent offspring to support at that time increased the likelihood that the condors would take a pass on laying a fresh egg. Snyder reasoned that if the adults were relieved of the worry of actually raising their late chicks to maturity, they might be induced to lay eggs more often. The strategy had been known to work with Andean condors, and it now worked with California condors. By removing the first egg and the chick hatched from the second egg, the team was able to increase the condors' reproductive output dramatically. Now, instead of producing one condor chick every two years, according to Snyder's calculations, a mating pair would probably produce at least two chicks every three years.

Capturing and Confining Condors

WHILE THE NUMBER OF SUCCESSFULLY INCUBATED EGGS IN THE San Diego and Los Angeles Zoos continued to soar, however, the number of adult condors able to produce them in the wild continued to plummet. Every year the census takers came back with lower figures. This decline was much more than an egg-supply problem; it also posed a tricky ethical issue for the recovery team. It was becoming increasingly clear that even with the egg- and chick-removal program, if left on its own in the wild the California condor would be all but extinct within two or three years. There would be a few captive-bred condors in zoos, but these would be condors that had never flown over their natural habitat, had never eaten anything but food given to them by keepers and had never found their own mates, defended their own nesting sites or raised their own chicks. They would be California condors in the strictly genetic sense only; in reality, they would be technically extinct, little more than living sacks of California-condor DNA.

Since there was no time to restore the condor's habitat, the only realistic solution to this futuristic nightmare seemed to be to capture the remaining wild adult condors and place them in the zoos. Then at least there would be condors left that could pass on what National Aububon Society (NAS) biologist Jesse Grantham referred to as "the condor culture" to their offspring. Fancifully put, the formerly wild birds would act as elders to new generations of captive-reared chicks; they would keep the condor traditions alive by teaching the young birds how to do the mating display dance, how to find safe nesting sites, how to recognize enemies and how to defend colonies. The old ones would pass on wisdom to the new ones. This was the theory.

OVERLEAF:
A tagged California condor from the Sequoia National Forest, in California.
MIKE WALLACE/LOS ANGELES ZOO

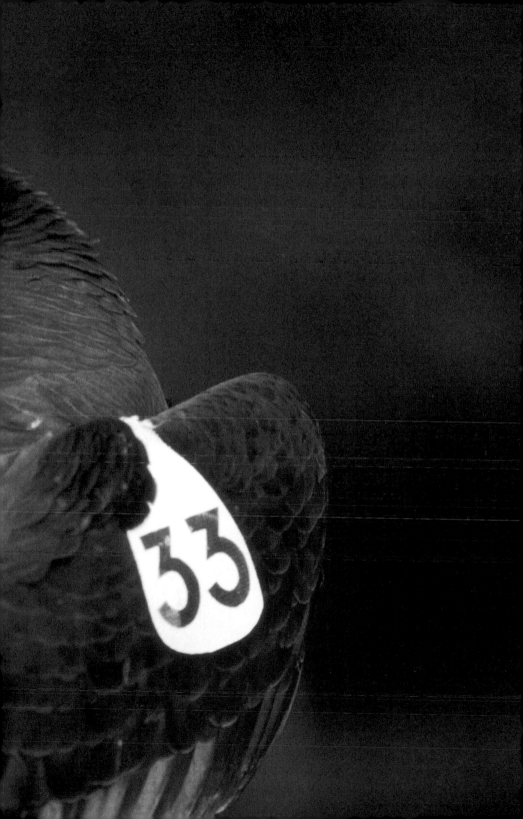

Capturing and confining adult California condors, however, was more fraught with ethical agony than any other part of the recovery program, and not surprisingly the team was split on whether or not to adopt it. Part of the team — particularly those connected with the California Fish and Game Commission — favoured capturing all six wild condors and placing them in the Los Angeles and San Diego Zoos; those working for FWS and the NAS wanted to capture three and leave three in the wild. There was no guarantee, they argued, that wild condors would breed in captivity or that if they bred their eggs would be fertile or that if their eggs hatched they would care for their young. Taking all condors out of the wild was too risky, they said — talk about putting all your eggs in one basket. Besides, since the whole point of the program was to release captive-bred birds back into the wild, wouldn't it make sense to have some wild condors already out there to act as guides? Then there was the political consideration: as FWS spokesperson Jan E. Riffe pointed out, placing all live condors in zoos cut the heart out of habitat restoration — they could hardly keep hunters and tourists out of condor habitat if there were no condors inhabiting it. It would be very difficult, argued Riffe, to protect California condor habitat under the Endangered Species Act if all living members of the species were being spoon-fed in zoos.

Between November 1984 and April 1985, six of the remaining twelve wild condors died, most of them from eating contaminated food. Although the wild birds nested within three national forests — Sequoia, Angeles and Los Padres — more than 90 per cent of their foraging area was over private land, where private landowners continued to shoot at them and also placed strychnine-laced cow carcasses out to kill coyotes and condors and anything else that came along for a free meal. The recovery team realized that it had to move fast; in August 1985, Snyder announced that the team would live-capture three of the six remaining wild condors, leaving the Santa Barbara pair and another male free in the San Joaquin Valley and placing the captured birds in San Diego Wild Animal Park. He also stated that they would release three captive-bred juveniles into the San Joaquin Valley within a year, restoring the natural number, and that the FWS had agreed to purchase the 5600-hectare (13 800-acre) Hudson Ranch, north of Los Angeles, to be preserved as a condor sanctuary for future releases.

Zoo workers feed a two-day-old condor chick using a hand puppet, to discourage imprinting on humans.
MIKE WALLACE/LOS ANGELES ZOO

This seemed a satisfactory compromise between the California Fish and Game Commission and the FWS and NAS positions, and everyone except the purists were satisfied with it. But then, in December, the Department of the Interior announced that the team would live-capture all six remaining wild condors and that that move obviated the need to buy Hudson Ranch. This announcement seemed to confirm Jan Riffe's prediction that live-capturing wild condors would make it difficult to fight for habitat protection, and when the FWS agreed with Interior that buying the ranch was "not essential," the California Fish and Game Commission's Brian J. Kahn, who had originally supported the capture of all six wild condors, withdrew his support of the program, and the NAS launched a lawsuit against the FWS to block the captures.

But the next month, in January 1986, one of the six wild condors died. She was known as AC3 — AC for Adult Condor. When the corpse was examined at the San Diego Zoo, it was found that she had been shot; there were eight shotgun pellets in her body. But it wasn't the pellets that had killed her. Despite the fact that a vulture's digestive tract can tolerate high levels of bacteria, condor blood has a particularly low pH count and is virtually nonresistant to lead poisoning. AC3 had ingested a single .303 bullet while eating a hunter-killed carcass and had died from lead poisoning.

In the spring of 1986, two wild condors in the Sespe Condor Reserve in Los Padres — AC8 and AC9 — mated and produced an egg, an event that ought to have been good news. But the egg was abnormally small, and its shell was so thin that it was crushed by the incubating adult: examination of its contents showed an extraordinarily high level of DDT. Opposition to the full capture-and-release program dwindled, although there was no joy on either side of the issue. Later in the year, the FWS finally bought Hudson Ranch and renamed it, perhaps aptly, Bitter Creek Wildlife Refuge. The last wild condor, AC9, was captured in April 1987. "Without a doubt," said Lloyd Kiff, the new recovery team leader, "our lowest point of condor recovery was bringing them in."

Releasing the California Condors

THERE WAS NOW A TOTAL OF TWENTY-SEVEN CONDORS IN existence in the world, all of them in captivity in the San Diego and Los

Angeles Zoos. Thirteen of them were hatched from wild eggs brought to the zoos; four were wild chicks that had been raised in the zoos; and the remaining ten were formerly wild adult birds that had been captured and confined. These birds were the species' last hope for survival, and they seemed a dim prospect. None were from eggs that had actually been laid in captivity. Seventeen of the twenty-seven were under two years old, leaving only ten capable of breeding. Of these, only four had formed mating pairs.

Nevertheless, success seemed closer when, the following year, the first egg laid in captivity hatched in the San Diego Zoo — a female named Molloko by the zoo staff. Molloko became an instant front-page star. The next year, four more eggs were laid and hatched, raising the total condor count to thirty-two and rising. Eight eggs hatched in 1990, and by the end of 1991 there was a total of fifty-two condors in captivity, nearly double the number that had gone in only four years previously. There were still no condors in the wild, but it seemed the species had been saved. For what it was worth, all of the captive-laid eggs that had hatched had been laid by condors that had once been wild; there was thus at least a sort of racial memory of wildness somewhere inside them.

The first captive-hatched condors were released into the wild in January 1992. Two were taken to Sespe, deep in the Los Padres National Forest, left in large cages for a few weeks to allow them to acclimatize to their new home and then let go. That fall, six more were similarly released in Sespe. All but one prospered — one of the January releases died in October from drinking antifreeze, although how she had obtained it was a mystery. But there were now seven condors flying over land that hadn't been marked by their giant shadows since 1987, and sixty-three more were waiting their turns back in San Diego and Los Angeles.

According to Mike Wallace, the Los Angeles Zoo's condor specialist —

OVERLEAF: Andean condors (*Vultur gryphus*) in Argentina often soar to 4500 metres (15 000 feet) and still detect potential dinners on the beaches far below.
GUNTER ZIESLER/PETER ARNOLD, INC.

known as Dr. Condor, Wallace had been closely involved with the recovery team since 1987 and has been its leader since 1993 — the team's long-term objective is to have 150 captive condors, 150 in the Sespe sanctuary and another 150 in various other remote wildlife refuges. In April 1996, however, when Wallace and Robert Mesta, a field worker with the Fish and Wildlife Service, announced

plans to release nine condors in the Vermillion Cliffs Wilderness Area in Arizona, a vast tract of ideal condor country contiguous to Grand Canyon National Park, opposition from local citizens and politicians halted the program in its tracks. After a series of public hearings and a lengthy comment period, during which Mesta received 206 letters — more than half of them favourable — the release program received local approval and was rescheduled for December.

The six birds released in Arizona and the seventeen currently in Los Padres bring the total number of condors in the wild to twenty-three, almost exactly the number that had existed in captivity barely nine years ago. There is now a total of 119 California condors in existence; the Condor Recovery Program has put the plug back into the condor gene pool and must be deemed to have been a success.

There still remains the larger and longer-term problem of habitat protection. According to Mark Palmer, a member of the environmental group Mountain Lion Foundation and a former activist with Sierra Club, the captive-breeding program has indeed shifted the world's attention away from the key issue. "They [the recovery team] have swept the condor's environmental problems under the rug," says Palmer. Continuing to look for new, as-yet unspoiled habitat, such as that in Vermillion Cliffs, is not the same as ensuring that previous wilderness territories be restored or even that future habitat be preserved. Those battles are still being waged, not only in condor country but throughout the New World, and no species will be safe until they are won.

A Satisfying Success

IN DECEMBER 1989, WHEN THERE WERE NO CALIFORNIA CONDORS outside the Los Angeles and San Diego zoos, Mike Wallace and a team of Fish and Wildlife biologists released thirteen captive-bred Andean condors into Los Padres National Forest. They were all females, so there was no chance that the birds would mate, and all the birds were later recaptured and re-released in South America. This program was an experiment. Wallace wanted to see how well the condors would do and to give the field team some practice in release techniques so that when it came time to reintroduce the more threatened California condors, they would know what to do and how to do it.

Wallace and his colleagues at the Los Angeles Zoo and the San Diego Wild Animal Park were fairly certain that captive breeding would work with California condors because it had already been successfully tried with Andean condors. As early as 1981, researchers had learned how to increase the productivity of captive Andean condors from one young every two years to as many as three young per year, by removing first eggs and, later, second-egg chicks from nests. Such high yields required regular releases to the wild, and Wallace had been involved in Andean condor release programs in the Cerro Illescas, in northern Peru, since 1980.

The Cerro Illescas, an isolated mountain range on Peru's remote Sechura Peninsula, is perfect condor country. High and dry, yet close to the ocean, the peninsula already had a viable vulture community: sixteen permanent Andean condors as well as regular visitors from inland, and a large number of turkey and black vultures. All the vultures procured most of their food from the ocean, which regularly washed seabirds and marine mammals onto the shore, and carcasses of wild goats and burros regularly appeared on the rocks below the high cliffs. Best of all, Wallace writes, "there was virtually no human activity within the hills of the Cerro Illescas." Two goat herders frequented the periphery of the area, and fishing boats occasionally landed on the beach, but the vast, mountainous reaches of the Illescas themselves remained untouched and unspoiled.

Wallace obtained eleven Andean condors for release from three wildlife centres in the United States: the Patuxent Center for Endangered Wildlife Research in Maryland, the Bronx Zoo and the Metro Zoo of Miami. Although hatched and raised in captivity, the young condors had not "imprinted" on their human handlers. Zoo personnel fed the chicks using condor hand puppets designed by Wallace, and great efforts were made to reduce human contact — the same precautions were later taken in Los Angeles with young California condors. When the condors were sent to Peru, they were first placed in large holding pens built on ledges right in the canyons and kept there from the beginning of June until the end of July. During that time they were fed local carcasses, and more carcasses were placed outside the pens so that the captive birds could watch wild condors and vultures feeding on them; the pens were a kind of condor restaurant, complete with condor television. Before

Threats
to the
Andean
Condor

• THOUGH A PROTECTED SPECIES, the Andean condor is not safe in all parts of its range. In 1989, a survey of the condor population in Colombia showed it to be on the verge of extinction in that country. By 1993, twenty-nine Andean condors had been released by RENASER, Colombia's Natural Resources Foundation, and in 1996, four more females were introduced: two in Chingaza Natural Park and two in Puracé Natural Park. All the released birds were obtained from captive-breeding programs in the United States, and by the year 2000 RENASER hopes to be able to sell chicks from its own wild population to other South American countries.

One of the countries that may be in the market by then is Ecuador, where prime condor country is under threat from developers. Ecuador's privately run Nature Foundation is currently suing the Ministry of Health for control of a 320-hectare (800-acre) piece of the Andean forest known as the Pasochoa Forest, in remote Pichincha Province, 4200 metres (14 000 feet) above sea level and home of a small population of Andean condors. Although the Ecuadorian Congress approved sale of the land to the Nature Foundation, the Ministry of Health sold 24 hectares (60 acres) of it to seven high-ranking ministry officials, who plan to build roads, hotels and restaurants for the 33 000 people who visit the forest each year. "It would be a lie to say that the Andean forest is in danger of extinction," says Nature Foundation director Teodoro Bustamente. "In Ecuador, it is already gone—except for a few tiny areas like the Pasochoa Forest. These must be preserved."

Meanwhile, in Venezuela, an active Andean condor release program is literally under fire. Following the successful release of ten Andean condors in two national parks in the central Sierra Nevada in 1993, local developers and politicians—including Avelino Villarreal, the mayor of the town of Mucuchíes—launched a fierce attack on the National Parks Institute in general and the National Condor Foundation in particular. Villarreal, according to *El Universel*, Caracas's major newspaper, claims that the parks program was "obstructing the plans of economic groups that are avid to develop large tourist centres in the region." Between May and August 1996, four Andean condors were found dead near Mucuchíes, deaths that Venezuelan senator Lucía Antillano attributes to Villarreal's anticondor campaign. The Sociedad Conservacionista Audubon de Venezuela has launched a massive letter-writing campaign, hoping that international support for the condor reintroduction program will help bring it back from "the brink of failure."

In South American mythology, the Andean condor symbolizes strength and endurance.

ERWIN AND PEGGY BAUER

being released, each bird was fitted with a radio tag, also designed by Wallace, so that its progress could be monitored; unlike most raptors, which need only a few weeks of postrelease care, young condors take months to become accustomed to life in the wild. For the first month, the researchers left carcasses for the young birds near the holding pens and then gradually moved the food farther and farther away until, after three months, the birds were ranging over a wide territory and had begun to integrate into wild condor populations. After 170 days, they were eating more often from natural carcasses than from those delivered by the researchers, and they were thus considered to have become totally independent. Although four of the eleven condors died from some undetectable sickness, the project was deemed a satisfying success: the Andean condor, though never numerous, is not a threatened species.

The Giant of the Andes

THE SIZE OF ANDEAN CONDORS CAN BE APPRECIATED FROM Michael Andrews's account in *The Flight of the Condor*. Andrews first realized how big the birds were "when I saw a stuffed one perched on the grand piano of the Director of the Chilean Academy of Music. It dwarfed the instrument." Andean condors can weigh up to 15 kilograms (33 pounds) and have wingspans of nearly 3.2 metres (10½ feet), second only to that of the albatross. Climbers who have heard Andean condors soar by on a mountain ledge — condors, when not incubating eggs or rearing chicks, are notoriously interested in human activities and often buzz climbers to satisfy their curiosity; and if they happen to frighten the climber into letting go, well, it would be a shame to let such an opportunity go to waste, wouldn't it? — say that the wind rushing through their long feathers makes a noise like a jet airplane, and indeed Andean condors often cruise on warm air currents at supersonic heights of 4500 metres (15 000 feet) or more. They are large enough to kill small or weak animals, such as newborn mountain sheep or llamas — Galo Plaza Lasso, a farmer and former president of Ecuador, told Andrews that he used to keep a condor as a pet until one day it flew back with a lamb — and they are also known to eat the eggs of seabirds such as cormorants and boobies, a practice that has made condors

Andean condors can cruise at great heights. Here, a group rests on a cliff face in Argentina.

PRECEDING PAGES:
Although not
endangered, the
Andean condor is
protected; many
captive-bred birds
have been released
in South America
from zoos in the
United States.
GUNTER ZIESLER/PETER
ARNOLD, INC.

unpopular among those working in Peru's economically important guano fertilizer industry.

But like all vultures, they prefer carrion; the larger and tougher the carcass, the better. As Mike Wallace discovered, Andean condors have no sense of smell of their own and keep a sharp eye on the activities of turkey vultures wheeling far below them, following the smaller birds down when they land and aggressively pushing them off their fresh llama or burro carcasses. Turkey vultures don't seem to mind; Andean condors easily open tough carrion cases that turkey vultures could not, and the latter have evolved a preference for smaller morsels and leftovers anyway, perhaps in response to two million years of competition from their larger cousins.

Like all vultures, Andean condors are voiceless — vultures lack a syrinx, or voice box, and can make no other noise but a hiss or hoarse rattle. But during the courtship display, when both sexes spread their black and white wings and strut purposefully about one another like fan dancers, the male will lower its enormous, wattled head towards the female and make a loud repeated *tok tok* sound, which its mate finds irresistible.

Like California condors, Andean condors lay only one egg every two years. Darwin was thus wrong on both counts when he stated, in *The Origin of Species*, that "the condor lays a couple of eggs and the ostrich a score, and yet in the same country the condor may be the more numerous of the two." There are fewer Andean condors in the wild than ostriches, and their molasseslike reproductive rate may be largely responsible. The chicks develop even more slowly than those of California condors — the parents support them with food for two years after they fledge, and the young do not reach sexual maturity until they are eight years old. All of which makes them poor candidates for long-term survival if the population is stressed.

Perhaps because the Andean condor is still a mythological bird in South American society and folklore, its situation is somewhat less precarious than that of its California counterpart. Its symbolic identity has survived more or less intact from ancient Incan times. A "condor" is also a Chilean coin bearing the image of the bird; the Andean condor is represented on the national crests of four South American republics — Chile, Ecuador, Bolivia and Colombia

Andean condors have no
sense of smell
of their own and keep a sharp
on turkey vultures wheeling far below them,
following the
smaller birds
down when they land and
ggressively
pushing
them off their fresh llama or
burro carcasses.

— Bogotá, the capital of Colombia, is in the province of Cundinamarca, a name derived from the Native word for condor, and Bolivia's highest merit award is called the Order of the Condor. "Considering the bird is a vulture," comments Andrews, "I find this choice rather odd," but consider the honour we bestow on the stork, which is also a naked-headed scavenger.

There are still several surviving folk customs in which the Andean condor plays an important part. In villages around Cuzco — the site of the ancient Incan capital in southern Peru — a mock contest is reenacted each year in which a captured condor is strapped to the back of a bull through a hole pierced in the bull's hide, and the two animals are let loose; the bull bucks wildly to free itself of the condor's talons, and the condor grips with its feet and jabs with its beak to get loose. This goes on until the bull tires; if the condor is still alive, as it usually is, it is set free. The condor symbolizes the ancient culture of the Quechua people, who once were subjects of the Incas, and the bull represents the imposed tyranny of the Spanish conquistadors. Every year the condor wins and is returned to its former haunts, like proud Natives released from colonial rule.

In the Callejon de Huaylas, a valley in another part of Peru, a different kind of ceremony takes place, one that has no obvious connection to Spanish rule unless it is true that colonial imperialism imposes a kind of suicidal death wish on the people it subjugates. The "fiesta" is known as the *Conorachi*, the "tearing of the condor." A living condor is hung by its feet from a rope in an archway, and villagers mounted on horseback ride under the arch and strike the bird with their bare fists. The lucky one who strikes the fatal blow gets to bite the tongue out of the dead condor and pay for the fiesta the following year — if he lives. Very often wounds incurred from bashing the condor become infected, and we don't even want to think about what can be picked up from biting out a vulture's tongue. This fiesta might better be called the *Venganza del Condor* — the Condor's Revenge.

All in all, the Andean condor has been luckier than its California counterpart; it ranges over a much larger territory, and it shares much of it with humans who still regard it as a sacred deity. Adapting a taste for seafood has also helped it to survive, a strategy unavailable in modern times to the California condor, which has to cruise the raked sand and posh marinas of the coast of southern California.

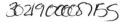

It is therefore sublimely appropriate that, in the 1980s, the Condor Recovery Team used the Andean condor to teach us how to save the California condor. Perhaps now the lessons we have learned from both these magnificent birds will help us to achieve a greater harmony with nature.

For all
vultures,
the word
"nest"
is always a ver
never a noun.
Vultures nest,
but they
do
not
make nests.

Andrews, Michael Alford. 1982.
The Flight of the Condor: A Wildlife Exploration of the Andes. Boston and Toronto: Little, Brown.

Bent, Cleveland Arthur. 1937, 1961.
Life Histories of North American Birds of Prey: Part One. New York: Dover.

Caras, Roger A. 1970.
Source of the Thunder: The Biography of a California Condor. Lincoln: University of Nebraska Press.

Darlington, David. 1987.
In Condor Country: A Portrait of a Landscape, Its Defenders. Boston: Houghton Mifflin.

Finley, W. L. 1906.
"Life History of the California Condor, Part One: Nesting." Condor 8: 135–142.

———. 1908.
"Life History of the California Condor, Part Two: Home Life." Condor 10: 59–65.

———. 1910.
"Life History of the California Condor, Part Three. Young in Captivity." Condor 12: 5–11.

Forsyth, Adrian. 1988.
The Nature of Birds. Camden East: Camden House.

Hilty, Steven. 1994.
Birds of Tropical America: A Watcher's Introduction to Behavior, Breeding and Diversity. Shelburne: Chapters Publishing.

Houston, David C. 1994.
"To the Vultures Belong the Spoils." Natural History 103 (9): 35–40.

Kirk, David A., and James F. P. Currall. 1994.
"Habitat Associations of Migrant and Resident Vultures in Central Venezuela." Journal of Avian Biology 25: 327–337.

Koford, Carl B. 1953.
The California Condor. Washington: National Audubon Society Research Report 4.

Turner, Ann Warren, and Marian Gray Warren. 1973.
Vultures. New York: David McKay.

Wallace, Michael P., and Stanley A. Temple. 1987.
"Releasing Captive-Reared Andean Condors to the Wild." Journal of Wildlife Management 51 (3): 541–550.

Wilbur, Sanford R., and Jerome A. Jackson. 1983.
Vulture Biology and Management. Berkeley: University of California Press.

FOR
FURTHER
READING

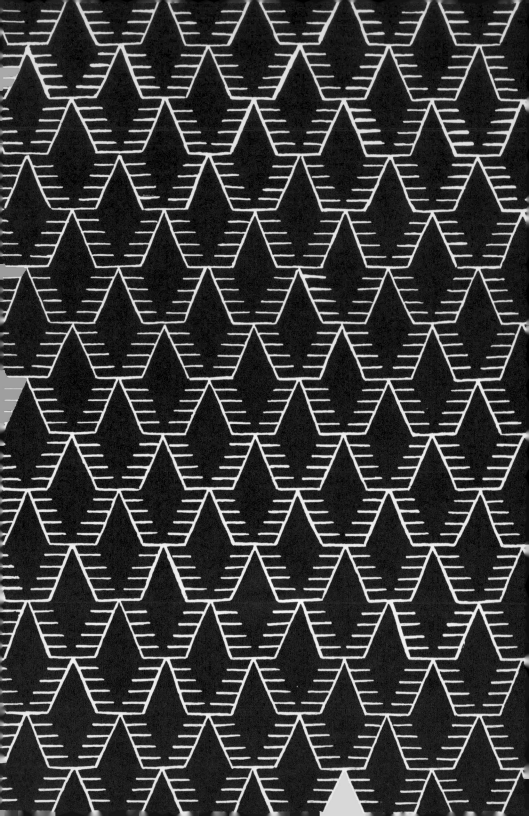